Fairy Godfather

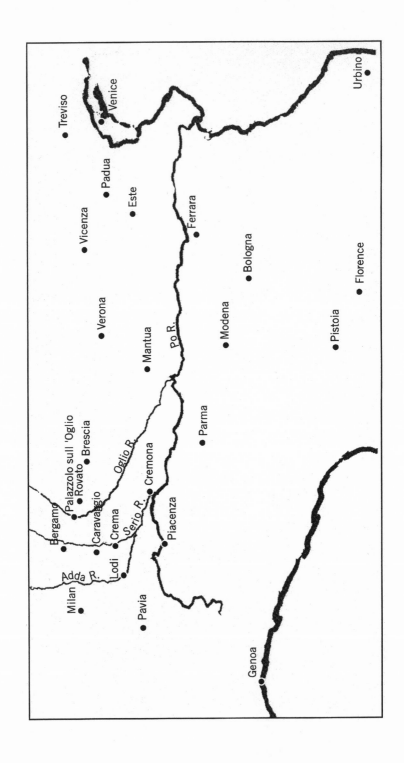

Fairy Godfather

Straparola, Venice, and the Fairy Tale Tradition

Ruth B. Bottigheimer

PENN

UNIVERSITY OF PENNSYLVANIA PRESS

Philadelphia

10   9   8   7   6   5   4   3   2   1

Published by
University of Pennsylvania Press
Philadelphia, Pennsylvania 19104-4011

Library of Congress Cataloging-in-Publication Data

Bottigheimer, Ruth B.
  Fairy godfather : Straparola, Venice, and the fairy tale tradition /
Ruth B. Bottigheimer.
     p.   cm.
  ISBN 0-8122-3680-7 (cloth : alk. paper)
  Includes bibliographical references and index.
    1. Straparola, Giovanni Francesco, ca. 1480–1557?—Piacevoli notti.
2. Straparola, Giovanni Francesco, ca. 1480–1557?—Homes and
haunts—Italy—Venice. 3. Fairy tales in literature. 4. Magic in literature.
5. Fairy tales—Italy—History and criticism. 6. Venice (Italy)—
Intellectual life—16th century. I. Title
PQ4634.S7 P523   2002
853'.409—dc21   2002020425

Contents

Illustrations

Introduction

FAIRY GODFATHER GREW OUT OF A longstanding fascination with an arresting distinction between two kinds of magic tales, those that restore position and patrimony and those that record a rise from poverty to wealth. Tales of restoration revolve around social position lost through misfortune and restored by goodness, perseverence, courage, or magic. "Cinderella," despite the fact that its title and plot customarily stand for rags-to-riches tales, is a restoration tale, for its heroine began her life in comfort as the daughter of a rich man before she was thrust from her rightful place by spiteful stepsisters and stepmother. The happiness of the tale's ending depends on the fact that the heroine's restoration surpasses her original social and economic level.

Tales that I have come to call "rise tales" recount different stories altogether. They tell of heroes and heroines who began their lives in real poverty, but who achieve riches and attain a throne, catapulted upward by a marriage mediated by magic.

In midwinter 1551 Giovanfrancesco Straparola, known among his friends and acquaintances as Zoan (sometimes "Zuan"), published a book of twenty-five stories, which he followed two years later by a second book with forty-eight more stories. Most were urban tales of artisans, the bourgeoisie, and the nobility, but folk narrativists have come to identify a number of them as "fairy tales": "Cassandrino" (night 1, story 2), "Pre Scarpafico" (night 1, story 3), "Doralice" (night 1, story 4), "Peter the Fool" (night 3, story 1), "Biancabella" (night 3, story 3), "Fortunio" (night 3, story 4), "Costanza/Costanzo" (night 4, story 1), "Ancilotto" (night 4, story 3, "Guerrino" (night 4, story 5), "Three Brothers" (night 7, story 5), "The Tailor's Apprentice" (night 8, story 4), "Cesarino" (night 10, story 3), and "Costantino and His Cat" (night 11, story 1). These tales should more properly be called Märchen, as Wilhelm Grimm called them in his little essay on Straparola in his notes to his collection. Although they are brief tales, as Märchen are,

Straparola's represent several different forms: nonmagical folktales, restoration tales that incorporate magic elements, and finally rise tales, in which magic is indispensable for narrative resolution.

It was Straparola's great and lasting contribution to the European literary heritage to have invented rise tales. For readers in his own day, however, the magic tales were just a novelty in a mixed bag that had something for everybody, ranging from Boccaccian urban tales to romances to reworked classics, all together in a book small enough to be slipped into a pocket.

Straparola's role as an originator in the history of the modern fairy tale has been recognized only rarely (Brakelmann 1867) and was ignored for most of the twentieth century. For the majority of the *Pleasant Nights* stories he demonstrably borrowed heavily from prior Italian tale collections. In cases where published prototypes are unknown, literary scholars automatically invoke popular oral origins. My position diverges sharply, for I have concluded, first, that Straparola himself invented the previously undocumented tales, and that he did so specifically for Venetian readers in the context of a generally faltering and occasionally recovering mid-sixteenth-century economy; second, that his newly invented tales were the first to address the aspirations of an urban artisanal readership; and third, that his new rise plot both anticipated and precipitated that plot type in subsequent collections.

Straparola's tale collection has been treated from a number of points of view. Literary historians have identified it as a component in the historical and literary development of the Italian novella (Dunlop 1816; Rua in Straparola 1908; Clements and Gibaldi 1977; Stocchi 1979; Pozzi 1981; Villani 1982; Smarr 1983; Guglielminetti 1984; Klotz 1985; Cottino-Jones 1994). They have also considered it in relation to medieval "commedie elegiachi" (Rizzardi 1989) and to Boccaccio's *Decameron* (Salinari 1955). The structure of *Pleasant Nights*, with its riddles (De Filippis 1947, Calabrese 1984) and its frametale (Barsch 1988), has also drawn attention, although to the best of my knowledge its songs have not yet elicited sustained interest. Scholars have investigated its publishing and translation history (Rua 1890a, b; Senn 1993; Ughetti 1981; Pirovano 2000, 2001), including editorial alterations made in response to the pressure of sixteenth-century censorship (Rua 1890a, 119ff.; Senn 1993). The *Pleasant Nights* has been understood as a putative record of oral tradition (Grimm and Grimm 1822; Mazzacurati 1971) and as a source for German tales (Hosch 1986). The fairy tales in the collection have been considered for their use of magic (Bonomo 1958; Demnati 1989; Cottino-Jones 2000) and as a test of Proppian theory (Larivaille 1979). And, of course, Straparola's gift of "Puss in Boots" to an ever-hopeful posterity has invited comparison between his version on the one hand, and Basile's and Perrault's on the other (Zipes 1997).

The three scholars who have devoted the most attention to Straparola's *Pleasant Nights* are Giuseppe Rua, Giancarlo Mazzacurati, and Donato Pirovano. Rua's painstaking research has provided the factual basis for most subsequent research. In September 2000 Pirovano produced an annotated edition of the 1551 (Book 1) and 1553 (Book 2) *editio princeps* of *Pleasant Nights*. By and large Pirovano and I had worked in parallel, consulting much the same secondary literature, but Pirovano's list of printings (2001) dramatically expands our knowledge of library holdings and carefully describes succeeding editions in exacting bibliographical terms. We immediately began sharing information, my contribution being the "fingerprints" (for details see Dijstelberge 1997; Vriesema 1986) of editions for which I had been able to record them. Pirovano's detailed comparison of alterations from one printing to another will undoubtedly provide the substance for future interpretive studies of Straparola's style.

In articles to date I've analyzed Straparola's compositions in their sixteenth-century Venetian context (1994) and studied those tales' dissemination with reference to print and oral routes (1993). In *Fairy Godfather* I examine Straparola's fairy tales, both rise and restoration, within the broad context of the *Pleasant Nights* as a whole, something that hasn't before been attempted. By relating hints buried in *Pleasant Nights* itself to the history of Renaissance Venice, I've also tried to create a possible, probable, perhaps even a plausible biography for a man about whose life little is known. In this effort, Katherine Duncan-Jones's recreation and personification of William Shakespeare in *Ungentle Shakespeare* (Duncan-Jones 2001) provides an inspiring example of enlarging what is known—or not known—about a historical personage by turning to ambient events. Her marriage of hypothesis to history affirmed my resolve to attempt a biography of surmise that was firmly grounded in and on historical record. In addition, I've tried to account for Straparola's working method by examining aesthetic, logical, and stylistic fractures in the collection as a whole.

Fairy Godfather builds on F. W. J. Brakelmann's 1867 conclusion that numerous modern fairy tales were first documented in Straparola's work.

Brakelmann's work has long been ignored both north and south of the Alps, in large part because it runs counter to an emotional and nationalist investment in the concept of oral transmission that colors most scholarly and popular treatments of fairy tales. Nonetheless, Brakelmann's dissertation remains as important today as when it first appeared.

The mass of secondary literature devoted to fairy tales in the nineteenth and twentieth centuries unquestioningly assumed—and continues to assume—oral sources for all fairy tales, despite the fact that a very different mechanism is suggested by internal evidence, historical conditions, publishing history, and the patterns, directions, and timing of the dissemination of rise fairy tales. These currents converge so unerringly on 1550s Venice and Giovanfrancesco Straparola's newly created tales in *Pleasant Nights* that I feel it reasonable to revise those long-standing assumptions and to ascribe the inception of rags-to-riches fairy tales to Straparola himself.

For primary data I turn to the tales themselves, as I did when I analyzed *Grimms' Tales* (*Grimms' Bad Girls and Bold Boys*, 1987). In *Fairy Godfather*, however, I draw heavily on historical conditions, the data of whose social, political, and economic history have made it possible to put Straparola's creations into a meaningful context.

The old myths of misty woods and dark forests have put the streets of sun-bleached Caravaggio and the tiny *campi* and broad open squares of majestic Venice into the shadows for far too long. Europe's first fairy tales about poor girls and boys who rose to royal estate and wealth with the help of magic and marriage did *not* originate with sturdy German peasant women in or on the edge of Germany's forests. Their Italian inventor was a Lombard who left home to seek his fortune in Venice.

The Italian and specifically the Venetian origins of the modern European rags-to-riches rise fairy tale have a history that has been intentionally suppressed. I hope readers of this small book will suspend disbelief for a few hours and join in exploring the tales and imagining the life of the lad Zoan Francesco Straparola, who took the name Giovanfrancesco when he created Europe's first "rise" fairy tales and put them into his *Pleasant Nights*.

One final word. Storytellers tell tales, and write them, very differently from one age to another. The tales I discuss here appeared nearly five hundred years ago in forms that differ from later renderings. To stress their historicity, I generally use the past tense to discuss them, rather than observing the convention of the narrative present.

I

Restoration and Rise

MEDIEVAL AND EARLY MODERN EUROPE was awash in stories that made people laugh, or that were meant to do so. Some were in Latin, the international language of scholars and priests, others in the regional languages that ordinary people spoke, such as Provençal, Bavarian, and Tuscan. The stories themselves were generally set in a town or village that a tale's teller and listeners knew, or knew of. The funny situations they spoke of—mistaken identities, deceptions, cuckoldry, wit, and rascality—exaggerated events that actually took place, or could conceivably have taken place, in daily life. The dramatis personae consisted of wives, husbands, sisters, brothers, priests, doctors, and merchants who were likewise drawn from daily life. In rough and raw humor, the body, its parts, and its processes were front and center. These stories, whether brief and jokey prose *facetiae*, vulgar verse or prose *fabliaux*, or longer prose novellas, often derived their humor from clever sexual deceptions such as feigned fidelity masking arrant adultery or from crude excretory humor.

Courtly romances and magic tales, whose plots were guided by elevated encounters and chivalric quests, described the plights of princes and princesses or of kings and queens driven from their kingdoms. Their subsequent restoration to rightful royal positions often relied on magic to bring about a happy end.

An entirely new kind of story emerged in Venice in the middle of the 1500s, when Zoan Francesco Straparola—as he was known—combined the urban tale's humble protagonists with the courtly tale's magic. First published in a handful of stories within the *Pleasant Nights* (*Piacevoli Notti*), their plots traced the rise of humbly born heros and heroines from poverty to wealth. For such boys and girls, it was not mother wit but fairy magic that led to riches. In terms of timing, poor heros and heroines achieved wealth in these tales *after* a royal marriage. Each of these tales of social rise followed the same pattern: rags—magic—marriage—riches.

The rise tale plot as Straparola envisaged it was altogether new to Europe's storytelling tradition and cannot be found anywhere in Europe before Straparola created it. In saying "altogether new" and "Straparola created it," I consciously reject a deeply ingrained and widespread prejudice against the concept of the literary creation of tales that have long been defined as quintessentially "folk" in nature. I do so, because no evidence supports that belief, despite the nearly universal assumption that authors like Straparola "appropriated popular lore" (Zipes 1997, 180), imitated "origini orale" (Mazzacurati 1971, 77–81 passim), or wrote down oral tradition (Pozzi 1981, 20).

Folk genesis of European fairy tales was a manufactured notion that nineteenth-century nation-builders desperately needed to support their shaky ideological enterprise. Jacob and Wilhelm Grimm, early spokesmen for German national unity, enjoyed high personal, political, and academic regard in Germany as well as throughout Europe. In addition, the Grimms' *Tales* had a foundational effect on the subsequent collection, presentation, and understanding of traditional tales from other parts of Europe. As a result, the Grimms' public espousal of folk origins for fairy tales gave enormous momentum to their view, which was maintained without being publicly questioned, until the Göttingen school of folk narrative research gave credence to book historical approaches to folk narrative in the 1970s.

Straparola's rise tales marked the beginning of all modern fairy tales that reassured their readers that even the most miserably poor boy or girl could gain enormous material wealth. In the pages that follow I will ask my readers to explore with me a novel way of thinking about rags-to-riches tales. But to do so, it is necessary to set aside three inherited concepts that have hardened into paralyzing orthodoxies.

The first concerns motifs, the basic building blocks of fairy tales. Motifs include objects (such as a tiny slipper or a spindle that sends a girl to sleep), magic animals (a speaking cat, helpful ants), stock characters (witch, stepmother, mother-in-law, king, queen), and standard actions (performing an action three times, being kind to animals). Associated with these motifs are familiar fairy tales that circulate in the modern world; mention of the same motifs immediately evokes memories of those fairy tales. Tiny slippers connote "Cinderella," and indeed, motifs like small shoes are identified so strongly with "Cinderella" that many people believe that the simple existence of small shoes in a piece of literature, even if that literature is one or two thousand years old, means that the fairy tale in which that motif now exists was circulating in much the same form millennia ago.

The second concept is that "the folk" has been the author, or the ultimate source, of all fairy tales. This has been said so often that even contemporary scholars often feel it necessary to affirm it as fact.

The third concept is a corollary of the second, namely, that the printing press contaminated the folk's stories by editing previously pure oral versions. The concept of contamination has been steadily weakened by historical studies of reading, authorship, publishing, and cultural consumption. Newly unearthed data convincingly contradict the concept of "folk purity" and "literary contamination" and at the same time undermine foundational thoughts about the folk authorship of fairy tales.

The three concepts outlined above have become articles of faith among most American folklorists and literary critics who work with fairy tales. And yet no objective evidence exists to support any of them (Bottigheimer 1989, 1993, 1998).

I've used the term "fairy tale" in the discussion of folk narrative scholarship, because it is the familiar one, but I'll avoid it as much as possible from this point forward because the meaning of "fairy tale" has become impossibly confused by its overlap with related genres and subgenres, such as wonder tales, *conte(s) de(s) fées*, literary fairy tales, burlesques, tales of origins, and folk tales. Each of these appears in the Grimm collection, where, in German, they are collectively called Märchen. Translators have rendered the term *Märchen* (which means brief narrative or report) as "fairy tale," principally because the Grimms *Kinder- und Hausmärchen* were translated as *Grimm's (sic) Fairy Tales* in fairy-mad nineteenth-century England, even though the Grimms' *Tales* for the most part had hardly any fairies. When American publishers adopted England's titling practices, they perpetuated the confusion. To avoid terminological problems, I'll speak of "stories," "tales," and "plots" rather than "fairy tales."

Stories and Tales

Stories and tales are brief narratives that communicate a sequence of events leading to a narrative conclusion. This simple statement reflects common knowledge and incorporates the ordinary experience of listening and reading. In terms of structure, stories and tales recount events in the chronological order in which they happened. Their sequential ordering distinguishes them from romances and novels, whose greater structural complexity both requires and produces greater length. Confirmation of this can easily be found in seventeenth- and eighteenth-century romances and novels that were simplified and shortened to create chapbooks for semiliterate or "simple" readers, as countless title pages called them. Abbreviation removed subplots from romances and novels, produced linear narratives, and resulted in cheap booklet- or pamphlet-sized chapbooks that peddlers sold in small towns and remote villages all over Europe. Editorial simplification turned complex romances into easily readable folk stories.

In traditional stories narrative events are composed of familiar motifs, but it is the way those narrative components relate to one another that creates meaning within a story. That is particularly true of individual motifs. Take, for example, three Grimm tales—"The Twelve Brothers," "The Seven Ravens," and "The Six Swans." They incorporate similar, sometimes identical motifs—a star, a shirt, a hunting king, fire, birds, a quest, wealth, the imposition of silence. They have parallel plots, but diverge dramatically from one another and tell different stories as the motifs in each tale accommodate themselves to the role ultimately played by the heroine. In "The Twelve Brothers," where the heroine is a pillar of strength in her quest to redeem her brothers, the star is a golden sign of royalty on the girl's forehead. In "The Seven Ravens," in which she is a weakened sister searching for her brothers, her star becomes part of the task imposed on her, namely the destination of her quest (sun, moon, and stars). In "The Six Swans," the star of a heroine reduced to a personally ineffectual little sister becomes an emblem of an impossible task. *This* ill-starred, treed, and silenced girl must sew shirts of starwort flowers for her brothers in order to change them from birds back into boys. The same shifts in significance are evident in the narrative functions of the three tales' other shared motifs: hunting king, fire, birds, quest, and imposition of silence.

Stories have protagonists, that is, heroes, heroines, and villains. It makes a great difference *who* does *what*, and *what* happens to *whom*. As I demonstrated in a content analysis of the Grimms' tales, gender is pivotal in characters' experience of speechlessness, isolation, punishment, and reward (Bottigheimer 1987). How such gender distinctions come about is a subject that has fascinated folk narrativists, and they have discovered close connections between narrators' own gender and the kinds of characters they have created. Such scholars have concluded, not surprisingly, that male narrators generally privilege male characters over female ones, and that female narrators similarly favor female characters (Apo 1988, Köhler-Zülch 1991).

Audiences, too, condition the way narrators and authors present characters. Numerous studies have shown that audiences, like authors and narrators, play a large role in the form a story takes. The same story may be told in a bawdy or a prim manner, depending on age, gender, and location. It is therefore noteworthy that Straparola's newly invented rags-to-riches-via-magic-and-marriage tales all have poor folks as their protagonists, a subject that I explore in connection with questions of Straparola's real and implied readership.

In Straparola's day, Italy, more than any other European country, was replete with stories. Schoolboys read *Buovo d'Antono*, and publicly hired municipal storytellers sang lute-accompanied romances such as *Historia di Lionbruno* in public squares (*Lionbruno* 1976, 5).[1] Giovanni Boccaccio's *Decameron* (1353), the structural model, the literary cynosure for authors of tale collections for more than two hundred years, and the preeminent Western achievement in the genre of story collections, was invoked and imitated in Italy (and all over Europe). His "honorable company" of seven ladies and three gentlemen (Boccaccio 1982, 5) told a hundred stories over ten days while they waited for the horrifying Florentine plague of 1348 to abate. The *Decameron* provided the style and some of the content for subsequent Italian tale collection editors and authors, such as Giovanni Sercambi (*Novelle*, 1374), Giovanni Fiorentino (*Pecorone*, 1390), Franco Sacchetti (*Trecento Novelle*, ca. 1395), Poggio Bracciolini (*Liber Facetiorum*, 1471), Masuccio Salernitano (*Novellino*, 1476), Girolamo Morlini (*Novellae*, 1520), and Agnolo Firenzuola (*Ragionamenti d'amore*, 1548).

Writers in other European countries were also deeply indebted to Italy's storytellers. One thinks of Geoffrey Chaucer's brilliant *Canterbury Tales* (ca. 1390) or the anonymously translated *One Hundred Merry Tales* (1526) in England. In France the Italian heritage was evident in anonymously produced collections, such as *Cent nouvelles nouvelles* (ca. 1460) and *Parangon de Nouvelles Honnestes et Delectables* (n.d.), as well as in collections by known authors, such as Nicolas de Troyes's

Grand Parangon des nouvelles nouvelles (1535–37), Marguerite de Navarre's *Heptameron* (1542–48), and Bonaventure des Periers's *Nouvelles recreations et joyeux devis* (1558).

Like his Italian predecessors as well as his European contemporaries, Straparola assembled many of the seventy-three tales of his *Pleasant Nights* from earlier collections. He openly borrowed twenty-three tales from Morlini's Latin *Novellae* and sixteen from Sacchetti's *Trecento Novelle* (Brakelmann 1867, 33–34). Other tales in Straparola's collection, not to mention numerous phrases within other tales, were inspired by the *Decameron*, while earlier versions of still others can be identified in lesser known collections. Despite his evident reliance on others' writing, Straparola stoutly defended the authenticity of his authorship. The stories were all "da me scritte," he wrote in an agitated response to criticism (Straparola 1553).

Straparola incorporated numerous tales of urban trickery into his collection. The characters in those stories lived in a zero-sum economy, where one person's gain was necessarily another's loss. Urban cunning outwitted urban innocence, and women bested men as often as men fooled women. Each cheated the other out of sex, money, and sometimes both together. But not all trickery was physical. On an intellectually elevated plane, one of Straparola's tales told how Bergamo townsmen scared off challengers to its reputation for an educated citizenry by disguising academics as roadworkers to greet and discourse in scholarly Latin with Florentine visitors (night 9, story 5).

In Straparola's tales, as in real life, the country surrounded the city and city dwellers were well aware of it. The country fed the city. The country absorbed the city's refuse. A remarkable number of Straparola's tales thematized urban/rural tensions, just as the frametale itself took up that subject: on the fourth night of storytelling, Straparola's authorial voice reminded readers that exhausted fieldworkers were sleeping peacefully in their beds as the mirthful Murano company of storytellers and their listeners assembled. Clever city dwellers pitted wits against simple villagers, or, in reverse, crafty peasants cozzened gullible citizens, as in one nasty example, in which a gullible city-dweller let a malicious peasant castrate him as a weight-gaining measure. Straparola himself evidently distinguished among the tales in his collection not only by their social and geographical location, but also by their urban or rural character, giving first Signor Antonio Molino's long urban tale in the dialect of Bergamo (night 4, story 3) and following it with Signor Benedetto Trevigiano's "peasant tale."

A distinction that neither Straparola nor subsequent scholars have made, however, involves story plots themselves. For students of fairy tales, plots propelled by magic are of particular interest. The subject opens an entirely different aspect of Straparola's collection to our view.

A significant divide exists among the magic tales in the *Pleasant Nights*, a divide that separates two kinds of tales, restoration tales and rise tales.

Restoration Tales

Restoration stories' heroes or heroines begin life amid wealth and privilege, are forcibly expelled from luxury into a life of squalor and struggle, and are restored to their initial status at the story's end. On the surface this looks like Tzvetan Todorov's ideal narrative which begins with equilibrium and proceeds through disequilibrium before returning to equilibrium (Todorov 1977, 111). Pairing and contrasting the restoration narrative trajectory with the course of a rise tale, however, relocates the course of action and places it firmly within a social context. In graphic terms restoration plot lines look like this:

Three tales in the *Pleasant Nights* are particularly notable for their restoration plots. Livoretto's long and complex story (night 3, story 2) told of his leaving his father's kingdom with a magic horse and of having to serve as swineherd, stable boy, and cupbearer before being required to transport to the Sultan of Cairo the beautiful Bellisandra, daughter of the king of Damascus. After Livoretto performed impossible tasks, the story took an unexpected turn, as the princess cut off his head from his body, and, having minced his flesh and cut his nerves into pieces and broken his hard bones into a fine powder, . . . took a large bowl and little by little . . . threw into it the pounded and cut-up flesh, mixing it together with the bones and the nerves, no differently from the way women make a *pastone* with a leavened crust. Having put the minced meat well mixed with the powdered bone and the nerves into the pastry shell, the lady made an extremely handsome figure of a man, which she sprinkled with the water of life, and forthwith the young man was restored to life from death more handsome and more lithe than he had been before.

When her aged royal husband begged her to try her skill on him, too, the princess "took up the sharp knife still wet with the young man's blood" and, holding her husband's head in her left hand, gave him a deadly thrust of the knife. But instead of restoring him to youthful vigor and beauty, she had his body thrown from the window into a ditch. Heartless, ruthless, and direct, Bellisandra's action freed her to marry the handsome Livoretto and make him sultan of Cairo. In terms of the restoration-rise distinction, Bellisandra's magic restored Livoretto to the royal status to which he'd been born.

Straparola's story of Biancabella (night 3, story 3) was nearly as long and just as complex as Livoretto's. Born the daughter of Lamberico, the marquess of Monferrato, Biancabella married Ferrandino, king of Naples, whose stepmother had wished him to marry one of her own unfortunately hideous daughters. When Biancabella gave birth a child while her husband was absent, his stepmother vilified her, falsified letters between her and her husband, and ordered retainers to take her into the woods and murder her. The servants, moved to pity by Biancabella's beauty and innocence, spared her life but cut off her hands and tore out her eyes. These they delivered to the queen as "proof" that they had carried out her commission. Biancabella, however, healed by a magic serpent, returned to Naples and magically built a palace opposite her husband's, a marvelous feat of construction familiar from *Thousand and One Nights*. The tale ended in a storytelling session much like that of the *Pleasant Nights* frametale itself, in which the magic serpent, now in her human form as Biancabella's sister Samaritana, took up a zither, and striking sonorous chords, told "Biancabella's story without naming her. Finishing the story, Samaritana stood up and asked the king what suitable punishment should be meted out to those who had committed so grave a crime." The king suggested a fiery furnace. Then Samaritana identified Biancabella ("Here is she without whom you cannot live");

the king recognized and embraced her; the stepmother and her daughters finished their lives miserably in the furnace; and "Ferrandino the king lived with his Biancabella and Samaritana for a long time, leaving behind him legitimate heirs in the kingdom."

Yet another, also lengthy, restoration tale recounted Prince Guerrino's adventures with a wild man (night 5, story 1). Guerrino's father the king prized his possession of the wild man, so when Guerrino freed the man from his cage, his father's wrath made him flee the court. There then followed wanderings aided by a mysterious and handsome youth, a good fairy, and a magic horse, in which the prince overcame ferocious beasts that were devastating the countryside and helped a honeybee, who returned the favor by identifying the hero's true bride, Potentiana. The tale ended when Guerrino married her and inherited the kingdom of Sicily, thus restoring him to the royal estate to which he had been born.

Neither Livoretto's nor Guerrino's story had a villainous antagonist. The sultan Livoretto's beloved Bellisandra dispatched so efficiently certainly was not wicked. Wise, wealthy, and powerful, his sole transgression was his extreme age, for which his bride murdered him in cold blood. Lacking an evil antagonist, Straparola produced narrative tension in his restoration story plots by introducing death-defying adventures whose dangers the tales' heros surmounted with the aid of magic animals and benevolent helpers.

Of the three restoration tales discussed here, Biancabella's story (night 3, story 3) stands out as an early example of gender differentiation in magic tales. Lacking the quickwittedness of her narrative sister Bellisandra (night 3, story 2), Biancabella, when mutilated, did not independently and intentionally determine her destiny, but suffered in isolation. Only when her sweet nature awakened the fatherly pity of a good old man did she find the instrument of her salvation. Suffering rather than acting, Biancabella foreshadowed the characteristic female experiences of the Grimms' heroines.

Rags-to-Riches and Rise Tales

In the European storytelling tradition two plots exist in which poor boys and girls become wealthy. The older of the two is a straightforward rags-to-riches tale; the newer is a rise tale. Both have heroes and heroines who begin their lives and their narrative trajectory in a low estate and end their lives and their stories ennobled and enriched. Rendered graphically, the social level of their heroes and heroines rises steadily:

Although rags-to-riches and rise tales have the same beginning (poverty) and end (wealth),[2] the means by which their protagonists rise differs fundamentally. The upward mobility of heroes and heroines in rags-to-riches tales generally hinges on wit or happenstance, which delivers one person's fortune into the hands of another.

The English tale of Dick Whittington and his cat exemplifies rags-to-riches tales. Whittington's cat eradicated mice from a catless oriental kingdom, filling his belly and preparing the way for his owner's acquisition of wealth in the process. Enriched by the grateful sultan, Whittington returned home, wedded a fine wife, and became thrice Lord Mayor of London. The tale exaggerated a cat's capacity for eating mice, but magic per se was absent: Dick Whittington's cat enacted catness pure and simple, although admittedly to a remarkable degree. It is significant that Dick Whittington's enrichment preceded his marriage, while his elevation was not to kingship, but to a real municipal position in the real English world in which both Whittington and his latter day readers lived.

In rise tales, on the other hand, magic typically precedes marriage. It is magic that makes marriage possible. The marriage is always to royalty. And finally it is marriage that produces money—not as with Dick Whittington, where money makes it possible for him to marry well and become thrice Lord Mayor of London.

Straparola's Costantino Fortunato (night 11, story 1) began his life in grinding poverty, but experienced magic through which he married a princess and gained great wealth. No trace of this story existed before Straparola invented it for the second book of his tale collection. It was, and was meant to be, a tale of social rise, as Straparola emphasized in the opening paragraph:

Often, dear ladies, one sees a wealthy man fall into extreme poverty, and one who is in absolute penury rise to high estate. The latter befell a poor fellow, who from beggary achieved royal estate.

Costantino, surnamed Fortunato, had inherited only a cat from his penniless mother, but Straparola's cat was no ordinary puss: she was a fairy in disguise who assured her young master that she would provide for his sustenance and his well-being.

Costantino's magic cat ingratiated herself and her owner with the king by bringing him gifts from her master, whom she declared was virtuous, good-looking, and powerful. Actually "Messer" Costantino was not good-looking at all. Like many of the poor in Renaissance Italy he suffered from the emblems of his poverty—in his case it was rough, diseased, and blotchy skin. To cleanse Costantino of his blemishes, the cat licked him from top to toe until he was clean and handsome. Only then was he ready to meet king and courtiers.

Costantino also lacked clothing proper for an introduction at court. And so the fairy cat stripped him of his rags and got him into a river just before the king passed by in his coach. Shouting "robbery" and "attempted murder," the cat alleged that Messer Costantino had been on his way to present the king with a rich gift of jewels when robbers had attacked him, carried off the treasure, and left him for dead. The cat's ruse delighted the king, and the idea that he was to have benefitted from the "wealthy" Costantino's rich gifts moved him without further ado to marry his daughter to him and to dower her with gold, jewels, and fine clothing.

Costantino's marriage elevated him into a coach, from which vantage point he was able—through the magic cat—to provide first the appearance of vast dominions and then the reality of a castle. Beneficent good fortune made Costantino's possession of the castle a reality when its true owner died in a distant accident. Soon afterward, a second death, that of his wife's royal father (to whom, in whose final moments, Straparola punningly applied an appropriate name "Moranda" adopted from current romances) made Costantino Fortunato king by acclamation. Ever conscious of the novelty of his signature plot, Straparola repeated at the story's end that he had told a rise tale, namely, that by his marriage to the daughter of the late king of Bohemia, "Costantino rose from poverty and beggary and became a lord and king."

The bare bones of the story of Costantino and his cat show that Straparola had perfected the formulaic plot of the rise tale—rags-magic-marriage-riches. Costantino and his cat survived not only as the "Puss in Boots" of many subsequent authors (see chapter 5); the story was also paradigmatic for modern rise tales. Its hero was the youngest of three brothers, the two elder of whom were mean-minded and stingy. The cat's magic nature was writ large and clear. ("Now it so happened that this cat of Costantino's was a fairy in disguise," Straparola stated early on.) Straparola also embedded a long-enduring motif, a mother's deathbed transfer of hidden magical powers to a chosen child.

In "Costantino and His Cat," as in many later magic tales, the transfer of magical powers turned into salvational agency, revealed in the mother's name, Soriana. It encoded her catness; the Italian adjective "soriano" refers exclusively to cats with coats of gray mixed with black (Gayraud in Straparola 1999, 509n1). And it was Costantino's gray "soriana" cat who became the exclusive agent of his rise to wealth.

"Costantino and His Cat" had a basic story to tell, and it did so efficiently: it was less than a third the length of Straparola's restoration tales. Moreover, its Bohemian setting must have been as exotic a location for his Italian readers as it would be for Shakespeare's English audience fifty years later. Here, as in all his magic tales, magic was a distant phenomenon, not something its readers could expect to occur in the Venice of their daily lives.

Costantino, despite his flawed character, was far more virtuous than the heroes in Straparola's earlier magic tales. His chief failing, hardly a serious one, was refusing to share with his brothers the meat and drink his cat smuggled to him from the palace dining room. In this respect he simply behaved as his brothers themselves had already done. Costantino's character in other respects anticipated that of the Grimms' heroes. Notably passive, he did nothing to bring about his good fortune. Instead, he compliantly followed his cat's directions:

> "My lord, master, if you will do what I tell you, in a short time you'll be rich."
> "And how" said *il patrone*.
> The cat answered, "Come with me, and don't try anything else, because it's I who'll arrange everything."

When the king asked directly how he'd ended up in the river, Costantino, in his agitation, "regrettably didn't know how to reply, but the cat who always stood next to him, answered."

In all Straparola's rise tales the moment of marriage was a key point, because marriage, or the marriage ceremony, immediately preceded a hero's or heroine's access to riches. Straparola scrupulously followed that narrative order in "Costantino": first the nuptials took place—with parental approval—and only then came the delivery of ten mules laden with gold and rich garments. The parental approval secured for the wedding in Straparola's rise tales represents another reference to social reality, for sixteenth-century weddings without parental approval were invalid and could not be the means by which a marriage partner came into possession or use of wealth (Delille 1996, 286).

"Costantino Fortunato" fit the upward-striving hopes of Straparola's passive and powerless sixteenth-century urban apprentice and artisan readership perfectly. For them he invented a magic-mediated marriage as an imaginary escape from the all-too-real miseries of poverty (Cottino-Jones 1994, 135, 188; see also Demnati 1989, 120). Before credulous imaginations or before readers of all classes who were willing to be amused, rise tales dangled royal marriage as a narrative solution to a difficult urban existence, not, however, in Venice itself or even in any of the many nearby towns with noble courts, but well beyond the geographical limits of Venetian artisanal lives. In Venice such a class-leaping marriage had always been unlikely, and since 1526, when a law forbidding marriages between nobles and commoners had been enacted (Chojnacki 2000, 53–75), it had become legally impossible. Thus it is no accident that Costantino's nuptials took place in far off Bohemia, unimpeded by a century's worth of marriage-regulating by the Venetian Senate.

In the course of the following chapters I will continue to discuss the probable identity of Straparola's readers. In this connection I reject both the supposition that Straparola's intended audience was (principally) upper class (Mazzacurati 1996) and the conclusion that Italian readers of his day were few in number and restricted to an elite (Zipes 1997, 181). My observations are closer to those of Margo Cottino-Jones, that the context for Straparola's tales' was "a subworld" (1994, 189). Unlike her, I don't believe that it was necessarily one of "poverty and indigence." Instead, I think it was a literate subworld. After all, Straparola himself included one story in which it was taken for granted that a servant would carefully read the labor contract he had signed with his master (night 13, story 7).

It is important to emphasize the essentially urban nature of Straparola's rise tales. They were composed within a highly urbanized society for readers within that society. Straparola provided newly conceptualized literary provender for a public hungry for promises of a better life. In "Costantino," the last rise tale he composed, he offered readers a generally passive and mostly virtuous hero, for whom magic brought about a fantasy future of marriage and wealth.

Straparola's path to "Costantino," the original paradigm for modern fairy tales, had been a long one. His earlier rise tales show the route he took to his final success, a process that the rest of this chapter discusses in detail.

Straparola's Early Rise Tales

Although "Costantino and His Cat," in its latter day form as "Puss in Boots," has become a worldwide favorite, the rise tales Straparola wrote before "Costantino" are virtually unknown. For that reason, the remainder of this chapter will be devoted to abbreviated retellings of five of his rise tales. It is customary to present such material in an appendix, but precisely because Straparola's rise tales are largely unknown among students of fairy tales, it is desirable to present them in the main body of the book. My versions are not word-for-word translations, but accurate representations of their content in a colloquial English that approximates the breezy Italian of the originals. To give a sense of their Straparolean form, they maintain some of Straparola's stylistic lapses while smoothing out others.

The first rise tale Straparola composed cast a desperately poor girl as a heroine who would, like Costantino, rise from rags through magic to a royal marriage and riches. It was "Prince Pig," the first story of the second night of the *Pleasant Nights*' storytelling.

Prince Pig (night 2, story 1)

Galeotto, king of Anglia, and his wife Ersilia, although married for many years, still longed for the child they had not yet had. One day when Ersilia lay down to rest in her garden, three mischievous fairies decided to cast a spell on the beautiful queen. The first said, "No man may ever harm her, and she shall bear a child of surpassing beauty." The second added, "No person may ever harm her, and her child shall be charming and witty beyond all others." The third willed that the queen should become the wisest in the land, but that her child would look and act like a pig until his third marriage.

The queen became pregnant, and when her baby was born he had a pig's trotters instead of little feet, a stumpy snout instead of a sweet nose, and a thick hide covered with boar's bristles instead of a soft baby's skin. The king and queen were dismayed at his appearance, but reared him lovingly and educated him as befitted a prince.

As Prince Pig grew older, he would go out into the city, wallowing in puddles and rolling in sweepings. Then he would run home to the king and queen, nuzzle their silk robes and ermine cloaks, and smear them with mud and filth.

Eventually Prince Pig wanted to marry, but the queen replied realistically that no girl would want him, nor would any noble or knight marry his daughter to a pig. But the prince persevered until the queen was at her wit's end.

One day Prince Pig announced that he'd seen the girl he wanted to marry, the eldest of a poor woman's three beautiful daughters. The queen sent for the woman and her daughter and said, "Good woman, you are very poor and are burdened with three daughters. But if you do what I ask, you will become rich beyond your fondest dreams. My son wishes to marry your eldest daughter. Try not to think about the fact that he looks like a pig. Just bear in mind that he is a prince, and that after we die your daughter will inherit the entire kingdom."

At first the girl held back, but she eventually accepted the pig's proposal. At the palace, she was robed in silk, satin, and velvet, but the prince's filth repelled her and she repulsed him. When it was time to go to bed, she said to herself, "What am I to do with this stinking creature? Tonight, when he falls asleep, I'll kill him." The pig prince, however, had heard her words, and when she fell asleep, he climbed into bed and killed her with a fierce blow from his sharp hoof.

Some time later Prince Pig again begged his mother to get him a wife. Much against her will the queen procured the second sister, but everything happened exactly as it had before.

Soon the pig began to beg his mother to let him marry again, this time the youngest sister. For a long time his mother refused to listen, but he insisted and even began to threaten her if he couldn't have the third sister.

Eventually the queen summoned the poor woman together with her remaining daughter, whose name was Meldina. She said to the girl, "My dear, it's my wish that you take my son for your husband. Try to ignore his appearance, and think instead of his father and of me. If you're prudent and patient, you may yet be the happiest woman in the world."

Meldina was a poor girl who had nothing, and she humbly accepted the queen's offer. The queen cried for happiness, even though she deeply feared that Meldina might go the same way as her unfortunate sisters. But after they were married, Meldina accepted and encouraged the caresses of her stinking husband and survived the wedding night. The following morning the queen found Meldina lying in the mud-covered bed looking pleased and contented, and she gave thanks that her son had finally found a wife to his liking.

Eventually Prince Pig revealed his secret to his wife: he wasn't really a pig but a gallant and handsome young prince under an enchantment. He told her to keep his secret. Not long afterward Meldina gave birth to a beautiful and perfectly shaped little boy. The burden of keeping Prince Pig's secret weighed so heavily on her, however, that she confided in her mother-in-law. At night, she whispered, her husband became a handsome young man. The queen doubted her word, and so Meldina told her to come at night to their room to see for herself.

That night, the queen had torches lit and she took the king with her to her son's room. As they entered, the queen saw the pig's skin lying on the floor in the corner and on the bed a handsome young man in Meldina's arms. The king ordered the skin torn to shreds, and after that, Prince Pig never again took any form except that of a handsome prince.

With so fine a son and grandson, King Galeotto abdicated. Prince Pig inherited the throne and reigned as King Porco for a long time, to the great happiness and contentment of his people, and he lived happily together with his dear wife Meldina to the end of their days.

For the first story of the third night of the *Pleasant Nights* Straparola produced his second rise tale. Entitled "Peter the Fool" it told the story of a slothful, mean-minded, poverty-stricken, unkempt, and stupid fisherboy who became a king.

Peter the Fool (night 3, story 1)

A poor widow, Isotta, lived on the island of Capraia in the Ligurian Sea with her only son, Pietro, a fisherboy. Although Pietro went fishing every morning, he always came home empty-handed. Nonetheless, every day he shouted that he had caught boatloads of fish, and every day his poor mother, who believed her ears instead of her eyes, got out buckets and pails for the promised fish. For her trouble, her impudent and stupid son only made fun of her.

King Luciano, who lived directly across from the widow's cottage, had a lovely ten-year-old daughter, Princess Luciana. Every time Pietro cried out, "Fish, fish!" Luciana ran to the window and nearly died laughing at the spectacle. Her laughter made Pietro angry, but the angrier he got, the more she laughed.

One day Pietro's luck turned, and he caught a huge tunafish. But the tunafish, to his amazement, spoke to him and begged him to spare his life, promising in return to grant whatever Pietro wished. When Pietro, who didn't have a diamond for a heart, threw the tunafish back into the sea and wished for a big catch, the fish so filled Pietro's boat that it nearly sank.

Beside himself for joy, Pietro paraded through the streets, shouting as he always did, that he'd caught a lot of fish. Princess Luciana, running to the palace window, heard him and laughed loudly. This enraged Pietro so much that he ran back to the beach, called the tunafish, and asked him that Luciana be impregnated.

Pietro's wish was immediately granted, and soon the princess's belly began to swell. When her mother saw this in her very young daughter, she worried that her child had some dreadful disease. But the wise women she consulted told her that, alas, Luciana was going to have a baby.

The king immediately began a search to find the person who had violated his daughter. When he failed to find him, he wanted to kill her secretly. But her mother begged him to wait until the child was born, which suited the king, who had compassion for his daughter, his only child.

When the baby was a year old, he was the most beautiful child in the kingdom, and the king decided to try once again to find his father. He issued a proclamation that, on pain of beheading, every man and every boy over the age of fourteen must come to the palace on a certain day with a fruit or a flower, so that Luciana's beautiful baby could pick out his father. When Pietro went to the palace in his rags, he hid behind a door, but as the baby was carried down the long hall past every guest, he began to gurgle and crow, to laugh and reach out his little arms as he neared the door where Pietro was hiding. When Pietro emerged from his hiding place, the child embraced him.

With the discovery that Pietro was the baby's father, the king's hopes died, and so must Luciana and Pietro along with the baby. With a heavy heart the Queen agreed. However, she feared that the people would rise up against their king if the Princess were executed in public, and so she begged the king to cast mother, father, and child into the sea in a huge barrel. It would be a gentler death, she believed, and she and the king would suffer less grief. The king agreed, and Luciana, Pietro, and the baby were put into a cask with bread, wine, and figs. It seemed that their lives would soon end, and Pietro's mother died of a broken heart.

Princess Luciana, shut away inside the pitch black barrel tossing on the waves, was miserable beyond words, but Pietro seemed carefree. When she asked him why he didn't act worried, Pietro told her about the tunafish's magic powers, and she begged him to give her his power to conjure the fish. Pietro agreed, and she asked the fish for a safe landing, wished that Pietro be transformed into a wise and handsome prince, and requested that a stately palace be built, with a garden with pearl- and jewel-bearing trees.

In the meantime Luciana's mother and father decided to atone for having sent their daughter to a watery grave by making a pilgrimage. On their first day at sea, they came upon a magnificent palace on an island where there'd never been a palace before. Curious, they went ashore.

Luciana and Pietro recognized them and welcomed them, but the king and queen didn't recognize their daughter and Pietro, because of the changes the journey had made in them. Full of admiration for the palace and garden, the king and queen were eventually shown a magnificent tree, from whose branches hung three apples of pure gold.

Later, as the king and queen were leaving, the biggest golden apple somehow found its way into the king's robes. Then the gardener arrived and reported to Princess Luciana that the apple was missing. She pretended to be greatly troubled and ordered everyone to be searched including the king, because the golden apple was the most valuable thing in her kingdom. The king, certain of his innocence, opened his robes. Out fell the golden apple!

Luciana rebuked the king for having repaid her hospitality with theft. He, however, claimed innocence. Luciana responded in kind. Although she'd had a child, she said, she'd never been unchaste. Then she introduced her husband and her child, and explained the tunafish's magic.

The family were reconciled. Princess Luciana and Prince Pietro were properly married. And after king Luciano's death they ruled his kingdom together.

In his early rise tales, Straparola had not yet distinguished them as a separate genre. Consequently it is no surprise that in one of them, "Fortunio," he appended to his rise tale a restoration tale.

Fortunio (night 3, story 4)

Bernio and Alchia, who lived "in the furthest reach of Lombardy," after years of childless marriage adopted a baby called Fortunio. Later they had a child of their own, whom they named Valentino. When they were grown, Valentino one day called Fortunio a bastard born of a bad woman. Forcing an explanation from his mother, he learned that he was not their legitimate child. Her words were "dagger thrusts in the young man's heart" and he left home to seek his fortune.

Early one day he found himself in a woods, where he settled a dispute in which a wolf, an eagle, and an ant were arguing about the division of the day's catch. Grateful for his help, the animals granted him the magical ability to change himself into their shapes at will. With these magical virtues, Fortunio made his way to the renowned city of Polonia, won the assistance of Princess Doralice, and after many adventures earned her hand[3] in a joust against an ugly Saracen. They were married, and by the by his father-in-law gave him a large treasure.

Up to this point the story was a recognizable rise tale, but then Straparola returned to romance.

Embarking on adventures, Fortunio was carried off by a Siren. Doralice went in search of her husband, taking with her their young son. With the child's help, Doralice enabled her husband to escape the Siren's powers and return home.

Like the meandering courtly romances that were circulating in his day, for example, Boiardo's *Orlando Inamorato* or Ariosto's *Orlando Furioso*, Straparola's tale now veered off into yet another, though brief, adventure:

Fortunio took the shape of a wolf and "devoured his adoptive mother and his brother, as revenge for the injuries he had suffered at their hands." After settling his score, he returned to his wife and lived happily for many years.

Straparola's next rise tale appeared as the second story of the fifth night. The story's implicit references to sexuality and its heavy reliance on bowel functions for plot and humor demonstrate its close affiliation with earthy medieval *fabliaux*. Like the story of Costantino Fortunato, it took place far away in Bohemia.

The Magic Doll (night 5, story 2)

In the country of Bohemia lived a poor woman named Bagolana Savonese, who had two daughters, Cassandra and Adamantina. Before she died, she gave her daughters everything she owned—a chest filled with tufts of linen thread—and then she begged them to live together peaceably.

The sisters were poor in goods but rich in spirit and virtue. Cassandra, the elder sister, spun a pound of the linen with great care and gave the thread to Adamantina to sell in the market.

When Adamantina went to market, she met an old woman carrying the most beautiful and prettily made doll in the world. Adamantina thought only about how she could get the doll, and going up to the old woman, she said, "My mother, would you be so kind as to take this thread in exchange for your doll?"

The old woman took the thread and handed Adamantina the doll. Smiling and happy, Adamantina took the doll home, but Cassandra, who was dying of hunger, became angry and began to beat her sister. Knowing she'd done wrong, Adamantina bore the blows patiently.

Come evening, Adamantina took the doll into her arms and sat by the fireside. Using oil from the lamp, she began to rub the doll's stomach and back before wrapping her up warmly in some old rags and taking her to bed.

Hardly had Adamantina fallen asleep when the doll began to cry, "I have to poop, Mama, I have to poop." Adamantina woke up, got out of bed, took the apron she'd worn during the day, and put it under the dollie, saying, "Go ahead and poop." The dollie, however, filled the apron with coins!

Adamantina woke her sister up and showed her the money that the dollie had pooped. Cassandra was amazed. She gave thanks to God for not abandoning them and begged Adamantina's pardon for hitting her the day before. Then she took the doll into her own arms.

The next day the sisters stocked their house with bread, wine, oil, firewood, and everything else they needed. And every evening after that they rubbed the dollie's stomach and back with oil, wrapped her in the softest linens, and asked her if she needed to poop. Then she would answer "Yes." And she pooped lots of money.

One day one of their neighbors visited the girls and was amazed at all the fine things in their house.[4] When she came again, she asked them how they'd been able to furnish their house so well, when only a few weeks before they had been so poor. Cassandra replied that they had gotten everything from a doll that pooped money.

The neighbor, jealous of the girls' good fortune, resolved to steal the doll for herself. She told her husband about the doll that provided coins day and night and said she planned to steal it away from them.

At first the husband didn't believe his wife's story, but eventually she convinced him. She made a plan: he should pretend to be drunk and to threaten to kill her. Then *she* would pretend to be afraid and run out of the house, so that the sisters, who were very kind, would take her in. After that, it would be easy to steal the doll.

The husband and wife carried out the plan, and in the morning the neighbor returned home with the dollie. But for her the dollie filled the cloth not with coins but with a foul smelling pile of poop.

When the husband saw and smelled what had happened, he shouted at his wife, opened the window, and threw the doll out onto the street. There it was soon swept up by some peasants who carried off the street sweepings to fertilize their fields.

A few days later, it happened that King Drusiano was out hunting and got a sharp pain in his gut. Dismounting from his horse, he did what he needed to do. But since he didn't have anything with which he could wipe himself, he sent a servant to look for something. Coming upon the manure heap, the servant saw the doll and carried it to the king. Without the slightest suspicion of danger, the king took the doll, but as he put it near his behind to wipe himself the doll sank its teeth into his backside. It held on tightly and the king shrieked in agony. His courtiers found him more dead than alive and were astonished to see a doll with its teeth in his bottom. They pulled hard on the doll, but the more they tugged, the more tightly it held on, and every now and again the doll would claw his bells (*sonagli*) with its fingernails so deeply that the king saw stars.

The agitated king proclaimed that anyone, of whatever station or condition, who could remove the doll would receive a third of the kingdom, and further, if a maiden were to free him from the doll, he would marry her. A great crowd of people gathered at the Palace in hopes of winning the reward, but no-one was able to remove the doll.

In the meantime Cassandra and Adamantina had shed many tears for their lost doll. As soon as they heard of the king's proclamation, they hurried to the palace and Adamantina said she'd try to remove the doll. Standing in front of the dollie, she said, "My little girl, leave our king in peace and don't torment him any more." As she said this, she took hold of the doll's clothes and began to caress her sweetly. The dollie recognized the little mother who had taken care of her for so long, and suddenly let go of the king and jumped into Adamantina's arms.

King Drusiano took to his bed to rest up from his ordeal, and as soon as his pains had lessened and his wounds had healed, he married Adamantina; soon after that, he made a fine match for her sister Cassandra. They all lived together for a long time in peace and happiness.

When the doll saw how happily and richly wed (*superbe nozze*) the sisters were, and how there was a happy end to the tale, she disappeared, and no one ever knew where she had gone.

"The Magic Doll" was the last rise tale Straparola composed for Book 1 of *Pleasant Nights*. In the second book of tales Straparola included two more rise tales, "The Tailor's Apprentice" (night 8, story 4) and "Costantino and His Cat" (night 11, story 1), discussed above.

The Tailor's Apprentice (night 8, story 4)

In Messina in Sicily there lived a Maestro Lattanzio, a man highly skilled in tailoring. This trade he practiced in public. Maestro Lattanzio was also highly skilled in necromancy, a form of forbidden knowledge that he kept secret.

Maestro Lattanzio had a young apprentice in his tailor shop named Dionigi, who suspected his master of following a forbidden calling. One day Dionigi crept to the door of Lattanzio's chamber, saw him at work, and was instantly overcome by the wish to learn the arts of magic himself. He thought of nothing else all day long, forgot everything he had learned about seams and stitches, and lay about so dreamily, that Lattanzio eventually sent him home to his father.

Dionigi's father, a poor man, was deeply grieved that his son had displeased Maestro Lattanzio, and so he beat him and sent him back, begging the tailor to take him on again as an apprentice, to teach him well, and to feed him as he had done before.

Lattanzio pitied the father's poverty and agreed, but Dionigi responded to his master's careful teaching with yawns and disinterest. And so every day Lattanzio beat him bloody, which Dionigi bore very patiently, because every night he hid outside Lattanzio's door where he could watch his master making magic.

Lattanzio finally decided that Dionigi was so incurably stupid that he need no longer hide his necromancy from him. From then on he did everything openly. Dionigi now learned necromancy so quickly that he could do far more complicated magic than his master.

One day Dionigi's father visited Lattanzio's shop and saw that his son was no longer learning tailoring, and so he took him home. With great sadness, Dionigi's father explained that he could no longer pay for his son's apprenticeship, and so Dionigi must now earn some money. Dionigi first thanked his father for all the money he had spent and the trouble he had taken. Then he told him he had learned something else that would put food on the table and clothes on the backs of the entire family. Through the magic he had learned, he explained, he would turn himself into a beautiful horse that his father could sell for a great deal of money, after which Dionigi would turn himself back into his natural form and return home. But, he warned, his father mustn't give the bridle to the buyer, for if he did so, Dionigi would not be able to return home.

It happened that Maestro Lattanzio was at the fair that Dionigi's father went to, and when he saw the perfect horse, he knew there was magic in it. He changed himself into a merchant, returned to the fair with a great deal of money, approached the horse, peered into its eyes, and saw immediately that it was Dionigi.

After a good deal of bargaining, Lattanzio paid two hundred gold florins for the horse. Dionigi's father said the bridle was not part of the sale, but Lattanzio offered another fifty florins for it, and led the horse home with its bridle. Once there he tied the horse in a stall and thrashed him savagely every morning and every evening, until the horse was a very sad sight indeed.

Lattanzio had two daughters, and when they saw their father beating the horse so cruelly, they felt compassion and went to the stable every day and caressed and fondled the poor beast. One day they put the bridle on him and led him to the river for a drink. But as soon as the horse came to the river's edge, he leapt into the water, changed himself into a tiny fish, swam to the deepest part of the river, and hid. The daughters were amazed and went home weeping, beating their breasts, and tearing their hair.

When Lattanzio came home, he was enraged to discover that his horse was gone. And when he found his daughters weeping, he knew without asking that they had released it. He said, "Tell me, daughters, exactly what's happened, so that I may get the horse back."

The girls told him everything exactly as it had happened, and Lattanzio immediately went to the river's edge, took off his clothes, and dived in. He turned himself into a tunafish and chased the little fish. But the little fish fled to the river bank, turned itself into a ruby ring, and threw itself out of the water, where it fell into the basket of a lady-in-waiting to Violante,[5] the only daughter of the king.

When the princess returned to the palace she found the ruby ring and put it on her finger. At night, while she was wearing it, the ring suddenly turned into a handsome young man. When he laid his hand on Violante's bosom, he found two barely swelling breasts. She would have screamed, but he laid his hand upon her mouth, knelt before her, begged her pardon, and asked her to help him, reassuring her that he had come neither to shame (*contaminar*) her body nor to sully her mind. He explained about Lattanzio's magic, his own learning, his father, the horse, the fair, the bridle, the beatings, the little fish, the big fish, the ring, and now the bed.

Reassured, Princess Violante was moved to pity. First she rebuked him for his arrogance in coming into a room into which he had not been summoned, but then, "not having a heart of diamond," she agreed to help him, so long as her honor remained unsullied. Dionigi thanked her and at dawn he changed himself back into a ruby ring. After this, the princess often took the ruby ring out of her basket, so that it might take its human form.

One day Violante's father fell violently ill. When Lattanzio heard of it, he disguised himself as a physician and went to the king. After examining him, he announced that his illness was indeed a grave one, but that he could none-theless cure him in return for a single ruby set in gold from his daughter's jewel box. The king agreed immediately to Lattanzio's modest charge.

Lattanzio began to work the king's cure, and after ten days, achieved a full recovery. The king then told his daughter to fetch her jewels. Violante set aside the ruby ring that she loved best of all and brought everything else to her father. Lattanzio searched carefully among the jewels, couldn't find the ruby, and asked the princess to go and search for it.

The Princess returned to her room, cursing the day Lattanzio had come into the palace. The Princess's hot tears and deep sighs moved Dionigi to take on his human shape. He explained that the physician was his mortal enemy and told her not to give him into his hands, but instead to hurl the ring against the wall with all her strength.

When Lattanzio returned to the king, he asked again for the ring. And so the king called his daughter once more into their presence and pressed her to give Lattanzio the ring as a reward for saving his life.

As soon as the king had finished speaking, Princess Violante went to her room, fetched the ruby and returned. The moment Lattanzio saw the ruby, he reached for it, but Violante took the ruby and threw it against the wall as hard as she could.

As the ruby fell to the ground, it turned into a fine large red pomegranate that scattered its seeds. Lattanzio changed himself into a rooster and pecked at the seeds one after the other. But one escaped his sharp eye, and that one turned into a crafty cunning fox that crept up on the rooster, seized it by the neck, and devoured it before the astonished king and his daughter.

Now Dionigi returned to his own shape and told the king everything. Afterward, with the king's gracious consent, he took Violante as his legitimate wife and lived in long and glorious peace. Dionigi's father, too, became rich, and Lattanzio came to a miserable end.

As we have seen, the rise tale sequence charts a general path from poverty to marriage to wealth. Some of Straparola's tales deviated slightly from this trajectory. Adamantina and her sister gained *some* comfort *before* her marriage to king Drusiano, and Peter the Fool lived in a palace before his wedding took place. When one considers that Straparola can be said to have been practicing a new genre of sorts, it is not surprising that he tried different narrative routes to marriage and wealth. By the time he wrote his last rise tale, "Costantino and His Cat," he had worked out the formula that would guide modern rise tales.

Straparola's tales sold exceedingly well. The handful of new tales that promised access to wealth must have held out meaningful hope for a life beyond the poverty that surrounded and impounded all but a few of Venice's young adults. Straparola's newly created stories fit their aspirations perfectly. They were, in a very important sense, the inverse of real economic conditions, which the next chapter outlines.

2

Ragged Poverty and the Promise of Magic

As WE HAVE SEEN, EACH RISE TALE Straparola invented for his collection of stories began with the hero or heroine's poverty and ended with enrichment through marriage to royalty. Such a plot was an outright impossibility in real life in mid-sixteenth-century Venice. It is not surprising, then, that the happy ending should occur, not just in a distant place, but with the aid of magic.

Ragged Poverty

Each of Straparola's rise tales openly thematized poverty. Since no noble or knight would give his daughter to one so dirty and reeking as he was, Queen Ersilia told her filthy son Prince Pig he could look only among the poorest of the poor for a bride who might accept him (night 2, story 1). Poverty echoed throughout Prince Pig's story. The queen went to a poor woman (*poverella*), and then she said, "You are poor (*povera*)." She pointed out, however, that the poor woman's equally poor daughter, if she agreed to marry the pig prince, would rise in an instant from being a poor girl (*poverella*) to being a princess of the realm. (Straparola actually designated her position as the daughter-in-law of a powerful king [*nuora d'un potente Re*], but that made her ipso facto a princess.)

The same thing was true in "Peter the Fool" (night 3, story 1). Although Straparola repeatedly referred to Peter as loony (*il pazzo*), even after he had been transformed into a wise and handsome prince, it was Peter's poverty that was thrown into high relief at critical points in the story's plot: first when Peter caught his magic tuna, an event that juxtaposed the real fact of his impoverished condition with the implicit promise of magically mediated wealth; and second, when Peter begged the tuna to impregnate Luciana, again thrusting before readers' eyes the immense gulf between the fisherboy and the princess.

Straparola detailed Peter's poverty in other ways as well. Peter initially resisted the tuna's pleas because he had a greater need to eat than to talk (*aveva più bisogno di mangiare che di parole*). Similarly, when a man on the street and asked Peter if he were going show up for the palace paternity test, Peter protested that he was poor (*povero*) and clad in rags.

In "The Magic Doll" (night 5, story 2), Straparola expanded the vocabulary of hardship and again tied it directly to the story's chief protagonist, Adamantina. In the tale's opening sentences, he announced that he hoped to demonstrate "how a poor young girl was helped by good luck, and became the wife of a rich and powerful king"(*come una povera fanciulletta, dalla fortuna sovvenuta, d'uno ricco e potente Re moglie divenne*). The heroine's mother, just like Peter's mother, was a "poverella," and Adamantina's sister Cassandra similarly suffered from "povertà."

Having outlined his plot, Straparola deviated slightly from the rise tale pattern, in which marriage precedes riches, by having the story's magic doll give Adamantina and her sister enough money to enjoy the food of a comfortably situated family, a "ben accomodata famiglia." What, however, did their well-furnished household consist of? If we imagine velvet and satin, Straparola's list quickly disabuses us. The doll's money bought a modest standard of living, providing the girls with bread, wine, oil, wood, and other necessaries—enough to excite their neighbor's envy but a far cry from the riches Adamantina's eventual marriage brought her.

In narrative terms the doll was, alas, a finite financial resource in two respects. She provided Adamantina and Cassandra with several days' worth of coins, but her endless production of money stopped abruptly when their jealous neighbor stole her away. The doll performed her principal narrative function—to provide an opportunity for the heroine to meet the king, marry him, and become really rich—when she reappeared, magically and painfully attached to the king's behind.

If readers missed the significance of the story's sequence of events, Straparola repeated it at the end of the narrative: the doll had "seen the magnificent weddings of one and [then] the other sister" (*le superbe nozze dell'una e l'altra sorella*). With that accomplished, the doll disappeared again, this time for good. Marriage had completed what the doll had begun.

The fourth of Straparola's rise tales, "The Tailor's Apprentice" (night 8, story 4), exerted little influence on subsequent tale collections, largely because the pressure of Counter-Reformation censorship resulted in its removal from the corpus of Straparola's tales within a few years of its appearance. Like his other rise tales, this one began with a poor protagonist and proceeded via much, almost too much, magic to a royal marriage. As a tale, "The Tailor's Apprentice" is primarily of interest because it shows us Straparola fumbling awkwardly with the idea of the mechanics of social and economic rise. Here he stressed not the poverty of the young hero himself, but that of his *father* and the fact that the *father* rose "from being a pauper to being a hugely rich person" (*di povero grandissimo ricco divenne*) at the end of the tale.

Every one of Straparola's rise tale marriage partners was royal, and every one of their spouses began life in penury. To make a case for the fundamental differentness of Straparola's rise tales, it is necessary to demonstrate that the poverty of his tales differed measurably and significantly from the circumstances in other tales of the *Pleasant Nights*. That is easy to do.

Most of Straparola's tales were lifted from earlier collections and most, though not all, of their characters were urban and well off or noble and well off. The protagonists in the tales of the first night fit that paradigm: a wealthy gentleman and his son (story 1), a young scapegrace named Cassandrino (story 2), a clever priest who duped three robbers (story 3), a king, his daughter, and her royal husband (story 4), and a merchant and his unfaithful wife (story 5). The same was true of the second night, except, significantly, for the rise tale "Prince Pig."

In non-rise tales—those that do not interpose magic before marriage—a disparity in wealth and social station between a male suitor and the female object of his affections sometimes existed, but these stories' outcomes differed jarringly from the "happily ever after" endings that characterized rise tales. For example, the wealthy Carlo da Rimini (night 2, story 2) tried first to seduce and then to ravish a poor widow's virtuous daughter, but the story ended with her melting from his grasp with divine assistance. In story 2 of the ninth night, a prince loved a tailor's daughter, but both hero and heroine died at the story's end. The third story of the fourth night began with a happy marriage of unequals, King Ancilotto and a baker's daughter, but Straparola did not describe the girl as poor in the same way that he did in his rise tales. Her father was a master baker (*un maestro Rigo fornaio*), and at the story's beginning his three daughters were enjoying themselves in the family's marvelously delightful garden *(nel giardino, di cui a maraviglia si diletta-vano)*, an urban amenity that only the well off could afford.

Other stories in the *Pleasant Nights* confirm the uniqueness of Straparola's rise tale formula of rags-magic-marriage-riches. The fourth story of the fourth night tells about Nerino, the king of Portugal's son, who consorted with a nonroyal beauty named Genobbia. He won her, however, not by magic but by cruelly tricking her elderly husband and carrying her off to Portugal, where they lived together happily . . . but unmarried. In the third story of the fifth night the dirt-poor and hunchbacked Zambò married his master's comfortably situated widow in a union of markedly disparate estates, but this story, too, ended unhappily with Zambò's death and disposal in the waters of the River Tiber. Particularly telling is Straparola's fifth story of the seventh night, in which three poor brothers made their fortunes and later saved a princess; that is, they became wealthy without magic and marriage. The narrative consequence? They couldn't decide which of them should marry the princess. Nor do any of Straparola's other heroes and heroines in Book 2—when their backgrounds differed markedly from one another's—enjoy the happily ever after conclusion that he conferred on his rise tale heroes and heroines.

The plots and language of Straparola's tales suggest that he composed some and edited others in response to the tastes of a newly emerging reading public that could afford to buy stories. The buyership for Straparola's stories undoubtedly included many prosperous merchants and members of Venice's hereditary nobility. But in terms of sheer numbers the potential readership for his tale collection was composed principally of literate urban artisans and craftsmen, as well as their wives and other literate but not necessarily well-off women. The evidence for the existence of such a population lies in the circumstances of Venice in the mid- to late-1500s as an economically troubled city, as recreated by social and economic historians. Between 1550 and 1600 the population of Venice grew from a little more than 150,000 to 188,000. The new inhabitants were largely craftsmen—wool and silk weavers, glass, wood, leather, and jewelry workers (Lane 1973, 305–13; Rapp 1976, 22). Because many of their crafts were in the process of being industrialized, however, their real wages were deteriorating (Lane 1973, 332–34), with occasional rises during a few periods of prosperity. Recent scholarship has focused on the intervening periods of prosperity and has indicated that artisans might have more money in some periods than in others, but has not altered the view of a socially rigid hierarchy.

The historical vision of a contracting economy corroborates the vision of scarcity and of often-hungry stomachs Straparola's tales convey. Messer Simplicio (night 2, story 5) pondered the honor of the virtuous married woman he wished to seduce and priced it at two capons. His conclusion implicitly and powerfully suggests that a good meal of fattened fowl would tempt even the most chaste of matrons.

Messer Simplicio's reasoning about the lady he lusted after corroborated values Straparola expressed in other stories, where he repeatedly used food as a narrative lure. In one case, the king of Thebes's daughter ensnared a satyr by sopping white bread in white wine (night 4, story 1). In the fifth story of the sixth night, appetite determined the plot, as a hungry youth succeeded in entering a garden, climbing a prized fig tree, and stowing the ripest fruit in his belly under the eyes of the watchman set to guard it.

In a faltering economy, food was a central concern. In one of his first stories (night 1, story 3), Straparola told his urban readers that a good meal for a village priest consisted of boiled veal, roast fowls, meat with savory sauces, and a tart. Ah, the joys of a full belly! In another tale, Cimarosta wagered with a Roman prelate for a meal (night 7, story 3). Even when describing a king, in this case "Guglielmo, King of Bertagne" (did he mean William the Conqueror?), Straparola characterized him in terms of the food he could eat, laying out a royally suitable menu of capon, pheasant, and partridge, with possibly a bit of fine fat veal (night 13, story 12).

When Straparola or someone else (see Chapter 4) leafed through Girolamo Morlini's Latin tales to fill out the eleventh, twelfth, and thirteenth nights, he picked out more food-centered stories: Diego tricked a peasant out of some chickens to make a feast for his friends (night 13, story 2) and a peasant experienced roast meats and tarts as "sumptuous" (night 13, story 8).

The social distance between rich and poor was immense in the historical Venice of the mid-1500s, and in the countryside outside, land was slowly passing from peasant hands to urban owners. Straparola's stories bear clearest witness to conditions in the countryside (Piejus 1976, 144) when Cecato Rabboso's wife enumerated them in sharp detail in Paduan dialect to the city slicker who wanted to bed her (night 5, story 4):

You're a Paduan, and I'm a countrywoman. You're a rich man, and I'm a poor woman; you read, and I'm a working woman; you're the chosen, and I'm the rejected. You're grand with your embroidered surcoat, and your patterned hose, all worked with wool and silk, and I, as you see, have nothing but a dimity petticoat, old, torn, and mended. All I have to wear when I go to a dance on a feast day is this old dress and this linen kerchief. You eat wheaten loaves, and I rye bread and sorghum and polenta, *and even then I don't have as much as I want.* . . . We poor in the country never have it good. (my emphasis)

In Straparola's rise tales foods such as Signora Rabboso's real world rye bread, beans, and polenta do not exist. In rise tales foodstuffs appeared in categorical terms such as the bread, oil, and wine in "The Magic Doll" (night 5, story 2). Costantino's brothers ate generic bread; his cat brought home unspecified "rich provender" (night 11, story 1). The only exception to the rule was when the king and queen provide Pietro and the princess white wine (*vernazza*) and figs with their bread (night 3, story 1).

The life stories of Straparola's heroes and heroines differ according to the tales in which they appear. By definition the heroes and heroines of restoration tales were born to privilege, luxury, and disposable wealth. For instance, Livoretto (night 3, story 2), son of the rich and powerful Tunisian king Dalfreno, set out on his adventures because his sex barred him (sic) from succeeding to the throne. He hardly left town dressed in rags like the heroes of rise tales, however, for on the advice of his sagacious mother his father provided him with money and jewels. Neither did the restoration tale heroine Biancabella (night 3, story 3) begin her life in rags or tatters. The daughter of a powerful marquis, she was born with a collar of intricately worked gold around her neck, and throughout her life she produced a stock of pearls and precious stones whenever she combed her hair. The much-persecuted children of King Ancilotto (night 4, story 3) began their lives royally, even though they enjoyed its comforts and privilege for less than a day. Another restoration tale heroine, Costanza, who dressed as a man and pursued adventures in foreign lands, was born the daughter of the king of Thebes and reared as a princess of rank. An unfortunate oversight had left her without a dowry and unable to marry a social equal as her sisters had done. Unlike her sisters, however, she had learned the arts of literature and the masculine skills of war along with the feminine arts of dancing, embroidery, and singing. Too proud to marry beneath herself, she left home with the avowed purpose of regaining her rightful social rank by marrying a man her own equal.

The wealth in which restoration tales' heroes and heroines began their lives contrasted almost painfully with the poverty of rise tales' protagonists. For the latter, poverty was a dismal state with whose details they had been all too familiar from the moment of their birth. In an economy of scarcity, readers who could afford to buy a book like Straparola's *Pleasant Nights* must have feared poverty as an ever-waiting hungry maw, ready to devour those who might—all too easily—slide into it. In such an economy, marrying into great wealth was just about the only way to avert the fearsome prospect of poverty, and that, clearly, could only be achieved by magic.

Magic: Actively Pursued and Passively Experienced

Alongside and in contrast to the existential problems of daily life, the magic in Straparola's tales offered a wondrous world of compensatory narrative. That position is advanced in Faouzia Demnati's study of the marvelous and realism in conjunction with their social and cultural implications in Straparola's *Pleasant Nights* (1989, 17–18). Demnati's work relates the manifest success of Straparola's tales—*two* separate printings of Book 1 in its first twelve months—to the promise of wealth and social rise that magic conferred in his stories.

In terms of the composition of his magic tales, Zoan Francesco Straparola may easily be understood as a widely-read assembler of magical motifs derived from stories that had been long known and enjoyed. (See Chapter 4 for an account of Straparola's working methods.) Reflected in his collection as a whole are plots and motifs not only from taletellers who preceded him in Italy, but also from world classics, such as Ovid's *Metamorphoses* (Clausen-Stolzenburg 1996, 137, 286, 334). It is enough to say here that some of Straparola's material can be found in Apuleius's *Golden Ass* and in medieval romances, in particular the Arthurian Round Table and Rolandian cycles composed by Boiardo in the late 1400s and Ariosto in the early 1500s (Brakelmann 1868, 34; Clausen-Stolzenburg 1995, 334–37). Some of Straparola's tales were simple reproductions of predecessors' tales; others provided a mix of borrowed magic and remembered might, while his handful of rise tales demonstrated novel uses for magic in the European literary tradition.

Straparola's magic itself drew on numerous magical traditions. "Prince Pig" (night 2, story 1), "Fortunio" (night 3, story 4), and "The Tailor's Apprentice" (night 8, story 4) all utilized transformational magic, the first to change its swinish hero into a handsome husband, the second and the third to win their heroes admittance to the beloved's chamber and later to overcome enemies. "Peter the Fool" (night 3, story 1) secured the services of a supernatural tuna fish by means of incantational magic, while "The Magic Doll" (night 5, story 2) produced money and *merde* responsively, as a measure of and reward for the true feelings of the person caressing her. "Costantino and His Cat" (night 11, story 1) referred back to animal speech, familiarized by Aesopic tales. Herbal magic in conjunction with achieving marriage is so strikingly absent from Straparola's rise tales, that it looks rather as though he intentionally avoided it in the tales he composed himself. For Straparola's readers, herbal magic was not fabulous but real; Venetian prostitutes and courtesans, for example, used it to bind clients' passions more securely to themselves (Ruggiero 1983). Straparola limited the use of magic practices common in Venice—herbs, divination, and compounding—only in the texts of his restoration tales.

With respect to magic, it is instructive to compare Straparola's tales with other tales of his day. Matteo Bandello's "Twins Nicuola and Paolo" of 1554 (Martone and Martone 1994, 77–114) included fairy tale elements such as twin siblings, a disappearance, forgotten love, a tale told about a villainess's misdeed followed by the damning question, "What does she deserve?" and marriage as the narrative capstone. And yet Bandello's "Twins Nicuola and Paolo" is in no sense either a fairy tale or in any sense a rise tale.

The same is true of "How Saint Bernard Was Tricked" by Masuccio Salernitano, the pen name of Tommaso Guardati (1410?–1475?) and of "A Trick Played by the Scheggia on Gian Simone Berretaio" by Antonfrancesco Grazzini (1503–84). Grazzini's trickster, in fact, was himself a teller of magic tales: "the Scheggia was an accomplished . . . troubadour of the most beautiful stories [who] . . . often told tales about ghosts and enchantments that delighted and fascinated his audience" (Martone and Martone 1994, 174). Bandello, Massucio, and Grazzini all drew on a common European heritage of magic elements, but they produced tales whose plots remained fundamentally unchanged from those that had been told in the past. Not one of them used magic as Straparola did, to hold out a promise of fortune before the eyes of the unfortunate.

Magic was crucial to the narrative outcome of Straparola's tales, whether it appeared in a restoration or a rise tale. And magic took similar forms in both types of tales. At the most fantastic level, Straparola's magic repaired anatomical damage and restored physiological function: medicinal herbs returned Biancabella's eyes and rejoined her severed hands to her arms (night 3, story 3). In night 4, story 3, an arduously gained green feather revived immobile marble statues, making them once again living creatures of flesh and blood. A magic potion in the fourth story of the first night enabled anyone who took it to live without nourishment.

Tripled acts have a long history and they also appeared in Straparola's tales. One heroine produced a palace of surpassing splendor by striking the ground three times (night 3, story 3), just as her predecessor had done in *1001 Nights* and as her successor would do in Mme d'Aulnoy's collection.

Straparolean fairies, who had stepped from the pages of Arthurian romances and like them had lives of their own, independent of the earthly beings whose happiness they helped or hindered, inhabited both restoration and rise tales. One restoration tale fairy, whose painful thoracic abscess was cured by a frightful-looking wild man, gratefully transformed the monstrous fellow "into the fairest, the wisest, and the most graceful youth that may anywhere be found" (night 5, story 1). Another fairy, this one in a rise tale, was responsible for the decree that Prince Pig (night 2, story 1) couldn't be handsome until he'd married three times. The most influential fairy in terms of the European literary tradition, of course, was to be the rise tale one disguised within Costantino's talented cat (night 11, story 1).

The most frequent magic motifs in Straparola's tales, however, were helpful animals who possessed the remarkable power of speech, and these appeared undifferentiatedly in restoration and in rise tales. A tunafish (night 3, story 1) could conjure up whatever was asked of him. Another fish (night 3, story 2) had three magic scales and its narrative compatriot, a falcon, had two magic feathers. The most dramatic magic animal in this tale was Livoretto's horse, who instructed his owner on standard fairy tale behavior. A small magical snake (night 3, story 3) accompanied Biancabella through eye-gougings and hand-severings, while a snow-white dove saved Serena's brothers (night 4, story 3). Three helpful animals—a wolf, an eagle, and an ant—assisted Fortunio (night 3, story 4). There was even a role for a helpful hornet (night 5, story 1) in Guerrino's restoration tale.

Magic animal helpers in Straparola's tales were chiefly concerned with *obedience* in those they helped, and when they encountered it they richly rewarded it (night 3, stories 2 and 3). Only in Guerrino's story (night 5, story 1) did an animal, the hornet, act out of gratitude for help given by a human—Guerrino freed a hornet mired in a pot of honey, and in return the hornet showed him which of two veiled princesses was his beloved. Western European tale collectors in the nineteenth century, Jacob and Wilhelm Grimm for instance, preferred that *gratitude* motivate animal helpers, because gratitude presupposed and proceeded from a desire to reward acts expressing a hero or heroine's inner goodness. In the Grimms' *Tales*, an animal's gratitude for a good deed freely performed doubled a tale's evidence of virtue—the first being the goodness in the hero or heroine's character that impelled the person to behave benevolently; the second the grateful acknowledgment of assistance freely given by the animal that had benefited from the protagonist's benevolent act. No one ever asked the Grimms and their contemporaries why they particularly preferred to reward gratitude, but the Grimms addressed that issue indirectly when they defined their book as a child- and folk-rearing manual. Implicit in their collection's normative intention was a powerful concept: a girl or boy or woman or man in a fairy tale who freely performed a virtuous deed did so without expectation of reward. And yet such virtuous behavior was *always* rewarded in their *Tales*. This narrative fact, surely recognized by fairy tales' readers, raised a hero or heroine's virtuous behavior to a socially normative level, while the gratitude expressed by the animal(s) confirmed the desirability of performing good deeds. In real life the built-in message to behave beneficently as often as possible propagated a model of behavior that was socially stabilizing.

Straparola, on the other hand, in no way viewed his tale collection as a child- or folk-rearing manual. On the contrary, he evidently conceived of his potential readers as people who vastly preferred amusement to instruction, and he must have recognized that if aristocrats were shifting from classical antiquities to marvels in their personal museums (Mazzacurati 1996, 146–47), then magic was a highly saleable literary commodity for the wealthy among his readers as well as among the poor. For him magic was a narrative device, not an invitation to morally or ethically desirable behavior. Consequently magic was not linked to morality in Straparola's tales. For example, in the fourth story of the third night magic won a poor boy a royal bride, after which more magic enabled him to take viciously uncompromising revenge on members of his family who had betrayed him. My account of magic in Straparola's tales is representative rather than exhaustive; many other examples of magic occur in his collection.

It is worth noting that magic is *not* gender specific in Straparola's tales. Men used the dark arts as often as women, girls as often and as well as boys. On occasion, each sex freely handed the use of magic off to the other, rather than holding tightly to it, either as a birthright or as a gender rite.

On a narrative level Straparola's magic was reliably effective. Straparola nonetheless allowed a second voice within his tales to comment, often skeptically, on supernatural goings on. When the golden apple from Luciana's garden (night 3, story 1) found its way into her father's robes, Straparola's authorial voice commented that it did so by unknown means (*occultamente*). When Straparola had to account for the disappearance of Adamantina's doll (night 5, story 2), he had the story's fictive narrator Alteria say, "Whatever became of it, nobody ever heard. But in my opinion it just disappeared as is always the case with phantoms." With equal skepticism the marquis of Monferrato (night 3, story 3) refused to believe his wife's story about jewels falling from his daughter's hair until he'd seen it for himself. Costantino acquired his castle (night 11, story 1) through the most mundane of causes: its owner, absent on his wedding trip, suddenly fell ill and died. Not until nearly 150 years later, when Perrault embellished the story by making the cat goad the castle's ogre-owner into transforming himself into a mouse so that the cat could gobble him down was it magic that would also provide a castle and retainers for its master.

Magic seemed to have limits in Straparola's view. Conjuring by the stars, by Scripture, and by magic herbs made a good show, but when it came to repulsing a marauder in the fig tree (night 6, story 5), throwing stones worked better than hurling incantations. Stones worked, because bodies were *real*. Sentiments like this echoed a realist's approach to magic and molesters.

Straparola's recognition of the effectiveness of stones against a fig-stealing youth paralleled brutal acts in the plots of numerous tales in his collection, where bodily violence was realistically, and horribly, inflicted by one person on another (night 2, stories 2, 3, and 5; night 3, stories 2 and 3; night 5, story 1; night 6, story 2; night 9, story 3; night 13, story 4). In other tales, sexual availability and violation appeared with an equally shocking vividness (night 2, story 2; night 3, story 2; night 5, stories 4 and 5; night 6, stories 2, 3, and 4; night 7, story 2; night 8, story 3; night 9, story 1; night 10, story 1; night 12, story 3; night 13, story 4), while one enigma after another, in their surface readings, depicted sexual organs and sexual acts.

In all the tales listed in the previous paragraph, the body was real and tangible in a way that affected the manner in which magic motifs appeared in stories. Straparola's era was an age in which the body of a criminal might still be flayed, whether he was still alive or already dead. The actuality of flaying, that is, stripping the skin off a human body, meant that the distinction between skin and flesh was a real one that many people had seen with their own eyes. Consequently, when Straparola's heroine Biancabella (night 3, story 3) was born with a delicately worked golden collar that was as visible as jewels seen through crystal, even though it lay between skin and flesh, its subdermal location would in all likelihood have been easy to imagine. Such heightened consciousness of the physicality of the human body would disappear from later magic tales, such as those by Mme d'Aulnoy or Charles Perrault. And for today's readers, the image of a golden collar between skin and flesh is inherently more startling than an image of a golden star on a heroine's forehead, a reformulation of physically embedded gold that both Basile and the Grimms preferred.

In the way heroes and heroines handled magic, however, a profound distinction separated restoration tales and rise tales. Restoration tale heroes and heroines dealt actively with the magic that was meant to return them to great wealth and high status. Bellisandra (night 3, story 2) eagerly flayed, chopped, mashed, and mixed her lover Livoretto into a paste that she refashioned into an even more handsome swain. Costanza (night 4, story 1), who had induced a magical satyr named Chiappino to reveal highly sensitive information about important people, gave him a sharp prick to make him repeat the same information to the king. And Serena (night 4, story 3) determinedly sought her brothers and restored them to life, while she and they used magic objects—dancing water, a singing apple, and a talking bird—to ensnare a wicked queen-mother.

Other restoration tales tell stories of collaborative use of magic, as heroes or heroines worked in concert with magical objects or people to benefit themselves. Guerrino (night 5, story 1) cooperated with a wild man who shared natural power and authority with a fairy and who also owned a magic horse. On quests and through tasks and trials, Guerrino followed the wild man's directions and behaved courageously. Acting in a manner that emphasized the peculiarly active nature of restoration tale heroes, Guerrino even increased his existing stock of magic power by releasing a hornet from a jar of honey and gaining one more magical champion.

Restoration tale heroines exerted themselves every bit as much as restoration tale heroes. Isabella, for example, actively sought out an experienced witch whose powerful magic helped her recover her straying merchant husband from the enchantment of a Flanders moll (night 7, story 1).

Passivity, on the other hand, characterized the way Straparola's rise tale heroes and heroines experienced magic. They didn't make magic happen; magic happened to them. Consider "Prince Pig" (night 2, story 1). In this, the first of Straparola's rise tales, Queen Ersilia suffered at the whim of three mischievous fairies. The first two blessed her and the baby she was to bear, but the third cursed the baby prince with a pig's manners and appearance. In other words, both the queen's body and the prince's body were acted *upon*, demonstrating that the motivational shift in rise tales affected not only the rising hero or heroine, but also some of the story's other characters. The same can be said of the story's poor heroine, Meldina, who for most of the story remained passive in the face of her husband's enchantment. Knowing that he lay separated from his dirty pig's hide every night theoretically offered several hundred nocturnal opportunities for her to destroy the skin of the fairy's enchantment. And yet she did nothing. Instead, Meldina communicated the prince's nightly transformation to her mother-in-law, the queen. She, in turn, brought the king with her to Meldina and Prince Pig's chamber, where—upon witnessing their son's magical transformation— the *king* ordered that the deforming hide be torn to shreds. His resolve, not Meldina's, broke the spell that had turned his child into a swinish suitor. The narrative resolution came from a character peripheral to the plot, the king. What had he done, after all, after fathering his unfortunately deformed son? To say that Meldina mediated the act by telling her mother-in-law begs the question, because it ignores the nature of her speech act. Her recounting of her husband's nightly transformation was neutrally narrative in nature and made nothing happen. It was her mother-in-law's initiative and her father-in-law's act that released their son. Although some would wish to see her revealing her husband's secret as an instance of independence, we must bow to the unyielding dictates of narrative logic and accept the heroine's actionless passivity.

The fact that the queen's body and Meldina's life were acted on by outside magical forces, whereas the king took action himself by ordering others to destroy his son's pigskin, raises the theoretical possibility that gender played a role in protagonist passivity vis-à-vis magic in Straparola's rise tales (Demnati 1989, 193–220). That, however, is not the case. In general, rising girls and rising boys remained equally passive objects of fortune's turnings and magic's transformations. The plot of "Peter the Fool," with its passive hero, well demonstrates that good fortune *happened to* a rise story hero. With glaring clarity Straparola's prose illuminated Peter's incapacity. On every page Peter's cognomen was "il pazzo," the idiot, the fool. In the story's first sentence, Straparola stated baldly that Peter "went crazy" (*impazzisce*), which nonetheless turned out for the best.

Careful intention and conscious volition are hallmarks of a canny heroine or a wily hero. Peter, blundering protagonist that he was, had neither. Take, for example the first real action in the story, the hero's catch and release of the magic tuna. Peter's sole intention was to fill his belly and to feed his mother, an expectation he twice repeated as he capered about delightedly (*Cenerò pur con la mia madre, cenerò pur con la mia madre*). Although readers may have grasped the fact that the magic tuna might bring about longer-term benefits, that awareness was one that evidently lay beyond Peter's mental grasp. He released the tuna because his heart was soft (*non aveva un diamante il cuore*), not because he comprehended the full import of the tuna's assurance that if freed, he would come to Peter's aid at any time (*ad alcun tempo agevolmente io ti potrei giovare*). In short, Peter the Fool had neither long-term goals nor intentions for whose accomplishment he would or could bring conscious volition to bear on the use of magic. When he begged the tuna to impregnate the princess, it was from personal pique, not from social strategy.

Pietro's lack of conscious volition was expressed in other ways. When he wished the princess pregnant, he did *not* say, "I want her pregnant." Instead—in a phrase that nonetheless conveys the same meaning—he expressed his wish as *not* wanting: "I do not want anything else except that nobody but Luciana the daughter of King Luciano should find herself pregnant" (*Altro per ora non voglio, se non che Luciana figliuola di Luciano Re, gravida si trovi*). In contrast, Straparola clearly implied the presence of volition of Luciana's part, when Peter said to her, "Your will be done" (*Sia fatto . . . il tuo volere*).

Those familiar with English popular usage should not be seduced into imagining a pre-Freudian slip on Straparola's part because the fish, rather than Pietro, impregnated Luciana. That is, it does not follow that Peter suffered from sexual impotence because Straparola conveyed the notion that Peter had no "will." Quite the contrary. The history of this story demonstrates unambiguously that a subtext of male sexuality in a brutally raw and angry form guided the story through centuries of retellings (Bottigheimer 1993, 268–70). In this discussion "will" stands for conscious volition pure and simple, and Peter had precious little of it.

Peter had as little power as he had conscious volition. He had commanded the tuna because he had the authority (*autorità*) to do so. Was Straparola making a joke about his own authorship? Was he saying that Peter could bring about Luciana's pregnancy because he, the author (*autore*) Straparola, willed it so? Perhaps. He certainly made it unambiguously clear that not Peter but the tuna had impregnated the girl, when he had Peter explain the magical workings of her immaculate conception (*Fu quello che t'ingravidò*).

Straparola's own words distanced Peter even further from any indwelling abilities his readers might be tempted to attribute to him. When Luciana gained control of the tuna, it was not because of her authority, but because she had the "power" (*potestà*) to command him. We may justifiedly read her "potestà" as an encoded reference to the absence of power on Peter's part. The likes of Peter the Fool suffered an enduring powerlessness vis-à-vis princesses such as Luciana, just as did nearly all Straparola's readers with respect to so unattainably an elevated object of desire as the princess.

In word choices like "autorità" and "potestà" Straparola revealed a fundamental contradiction between the real Venetian world outside his window and the narrative fantasy he was in the process of spinning for his readers. It was, after all, precisely the actual unreachability and unattainability of such a bride that his newly-invented tellings were meant to bridge imaginatively.

Peter couldn't—or didn't—make much happen in his rise tale.

Someone else persuaded him to go to the palace for the paternity test. He donned proper clothing, but in an unmistakably passive grammatical construction: to him was given a garment (*li fu datto una vesta*). Even well-clad, he hid behind a door. When his social rise, his public association with Princess Luciana, began, it was because his child identified him, not he the child.

The magic of "Peter the Fool" was not Peter's magic. It was wrought by "a fish named tuna." In a phrase Straparola twice repeated as his concluding narrative statement, it was he (the fish) who (*Costui fu quello che*) performed all the magic.

The supremely passive hero with whom the reader was left had also been poor and angry. Enraged, he had reacted reflexively, unthinkingly, and violently, expressing a limited number of emotions. With no sense of what he could have achieved using the tuna's magic, he handed over the small authority he had gained to Princess Luciana. Only in a series of wish-fulfilling events made by Luciana, that is, *by someone else*, did he finally become a handsome and wise ruler.

Straparola's Peter the Fool manifested many of the characteristics that Max Lüthi would later ascribe to fairy tale protagonists. With his two-dimensionality, he was far more a type, a crazy idiot (*il pazzo*), than a real person.

"The Sorcerer's Apprentice" (night 8, story 4), whose initially poor hero rose to a royal wedding, was every bit as much a rise tale as "Peter the Fool." But the tale occupied a different position on the spectrum of narrative variability because it differed markedly in its lexical variety, in the characterization of its hero, and in terms of the hero's indwelling powers. (For the plot, see Chapter 1.) Straparola summed Peter up in the single repeated epithet, "the fool" (*il pazzo*). Dionigi's narrative idiocy, on the other hand, was expressed in a broad variety of ways. He was not only "ignorant" (*pigro*) and "a know nothing" (*ignorante*), no longer "skilled" (*saputo*) or "industrious" (*diligente*), he was also "altogether a sleepyhead" (*si demonstrava d'addormentato*) and "a nitwit" (*gargione*) with "a plate for a brain that couldn't learn anything" (*tondo di cervello, né poter apparare cosa*). The reason Dionigi's incapacities showed now one, now another aspect of lazy stupidity lay in his character. Unlike Peter, Dionigi had been created "industrious and shrewd" (*diligente ed accorto*), a fellow who learned easily. It was not a lazy or stupid *nature* that made him a heavy-lidded dullard during the day, but his passionate nightly study of his master's exercises in necromancy that daily occupied his barely waking thoughts.[1] From what he observed, however, Lattanzio believed Dionigi to be so dullwitted that as master he no longer needed to hide his magic arts from his apprentice. With his master's arts open to his view, Dionigi showed himself highly intelligent as he learned quickly and effectively.

In terms of Straparola's characterizations, Peter and Dionigi were diametrical opposites. Where Peter handed over to Princess Luciana his authority to command the magic tuna, Dionigi used the magical powers he had learned to gain money for his father (by transforming himself into a beautiful horse that his father sold to Lattanzio at a fair). It was because his father didn't follow his son's directions, not because of his own ineptness, that Dionigi fell under the sorcerer's control. As captive horse, Dionigi achieved his escape when he tricked Lattanzio's daughters into restoring his enchanted bridle. Once in the princess's chamber, Dionigi continued to mastermind his magic. First he "put his hand on Violante's virginal bosom and found two young firm round breasts" (*messa la mano sopra il candido petto di Violante, trovò due popoline ritondette e sode*), and when she attempted to summon help, he put his hand "on her mouth" (*sopra la bocca*). His eloquence and sincerity won Princess Violante's sympathy, so that she willingly and eagerly collaborated in his victory over Lattanzio.

Dionigi, as the exception that proves the rule, is the most active of Straparola's rise tale heroes. It is interesting to think what effect a hero like Dionigi would have had on Italian rise tales if "The Tailor's Apprentice" had survived for any length of time.[2] But within five years of its first published appearance the story fell victim to the north Italian Inquisition's zeal to stamp out references to and belief in the dark arts of necromancy, and it disappeared from the *Pleasant Nights*.

3

A Possible Biography for
Zoan Francesco Straparola da Caravaggio

THE LIFE OF THE MAN KNOWN TO THE WORLD since 1551 as Giovan
Francesco Straparola is a nearly blank sheet. Only a handful of facts
document his life. In Caravaggio, where he began his life, he knew, or
knew of, Giacomo Secco, whom he later named in a sonnet. When he
arrived in Venice, he wrote himself onto the title page of his *Opera
Nova* as Zoan, a typically Lombard rendering of Giovanni. Forty-two
years later, in March 1550, he was a Venetian Zuan ("Zuan Francesco
Straparola da Caravaggio") when he received a ten-year privilege to
publish the stories of *Pleasant Nights*.[1] And in January 1551 he was a
properly Tuscan Giovan on his book's title page. The last fact we know
about him is that he paid for printings of *Pleasant Nights* ("ad instanza
dell' autore"[2]).

Straparola's date of birth is an estimate—sometime between 1480
and 1490—and his date of death—1557—an inference that I revise to 1555
at the end of Chapter 4. Only these few facts exist. Nonetheless, we can
guess something about his life based on the few known facts, clues
abstracted from his *New Works* (*Opera nova*) and *Pleasant Nights*, and
the rich histories of Renaissance Venice and Caravaggio. Providing a life
history, even if only a possible or a probable one, is small recompense
for the man who invented the wildly popular and widely beloved plot
of rags-to-riches-through-magic-and-marriage.

The title of Straparola's book of sonnets incorporated his Caravaggio origins into its title, *Opera nova de Zoan Francesco Straparola de Caravazo novamente stampata*, and in *Cremona illustrata* Franciscus Arisius
confirmed Straparola's origins on the Lombard plain.[3] Caravaggio was
an ancient town.[4] Although it existed in Roman times, its situation
on a slight rise that people called the "island of Fulcheria" amid vast,
miasmic marshlands did not invite Roman roadbuilding or habitation.

It took a thousand years of trenching, canalizing, and draining marsh waters into the Serio and Adda Rivers to make the land surrounding Caravaggio habitable (Secco d'Aragona 1968, 9).

In the late 1400s Caravaggio was a walled town of small merchants, artisans, farmers, and laborers. It lay about 130 miles (approximately 200 kilometers) west of Venice in the province of Bergamo, twenty-some miles (about 35 kilometers) from Milan. Two generations before Straparola's birth, Caravaggio had passed back and forth between Milanese and Venetian forces, and in 1447, by virtue of a pact between Milan and Venice, Caravaggio became a holding of Milan's ruling family, the Sforzas. Fifty peaceful years ensued (anon. 1991, 1–7). Thirty-five or forty years into this relatively serene and prosperous period, sometime in the 1480s, Zoan Francesco was born.

"Straparola" wasn't a family name but a nickname, a common naming feature in Italy in the 1400s and 1500s. The Italian verb *straparlare* means "to talk too much" or "to talk nonsense." Although "Straparola" isn't a standard Italian word, its meaning is clear: "wordy," "talkative," "loudmouth," "verbose," "long-winded," "big-mouth," "garrulous," "gabby," "expansive," "chatterbox," "prolix," "loquacious." The fact that this Zoan was distinguished by a nickname rather than by a family name suggests that he emerged from nameless, humble origins. Family names distinguished the wealthy and the powerful such as the Medici in Florence, the Scaliger in Verona, the Este in Ferrara, the Gonzaga in Mantua, the Visconti and the Sforza in Milan. In Caravaggio a prominent family was the Secco.[5] Three generations before, in 1401, Fermo Secco (1365–1401), his wife Florida d'Arco, and their children were memorialized on a sarcophagus built into the wall of the church of Sts. Fermo and Rustico.[6] Merchants, too, had names, and so did guild masters: in Caravaggio there were the Valeri, the Tadini, the de Prata, and the Ferrari. Caravaggio's most famous son, the painter who made *chiaroscuro* his metier two generations later, began life as Michaelangelo Merisi, that is, with a given name and a family name. But when he painted in Rome, he was known by the town he came from. The result was that—like "da Vinci" and "Veronese"—the town of his birth, Caravaggio, became the name by which he was known.

The children of humble families such as Zoan's were named descriptively. "Zoan the Fat," for instance, was sufficient to distinguish one Zoan from other local Zoans as long as the rotund Zoan remained in his native town or village. If he sought work in another—and usually larger—town, then he would need to be distinguished there from other Fat Johns—or in Straparola's case, Garrulous Johns—by adding the name of his hometown. So it was that in Venice Straparola became "Zoan Straparola da Caravaggio." His first name "Zoan," common in northern Italy in the 1400s and 1500s, was rendered as "Zuan" in Venice. If he had close friends, they might have called him by the diminutive form, "Zanni."

Straparola's parents were probably poor, because most people were poor. In all likelihood they were artisans, like the majority of the urban population in Lombardy in the late 1400s. They might have been intaglio workers, carpenters, cabinetmakers, coachmakers, silversmiths, tinsmiths, or knifemakers. Or they could have figured among Caravaggio's many linen spinners and weavers, or possibly among the town's small number of silk spinners and weavers, or even among the town's masons who were busy constructing the new church of San Bernardino da Siena during Zoan's boyhood (Santagiuliana 1981, 118).[7] They may well have had a small plot of land among the flat irrigated fields outside the town walls. If so, they probably rented it from a noble landlord, since at that time most of the land around Caravaggio was owned by the nobility (Anon. 1991, 10), among whom the Secco were the largest landholders.

In the 1490s Zoan was probably just another little boy in Caravaggio with a more or less ordinary mother and father. Like those of his playmates and like everyone else, his everyday meals included *pane di mistura*, a dark bread whose flour was ground in communal mills, with white bread reserved for holidays (Santagiuliana 1981, 112–14, 116). For variety there would have been vegetables and occasional fruit, while a foray into the country round about would have netted fish, frogs, and perhaps a duck or two from the willow-lined irrigation canals (Santagiuliana 1981, 112).

As soon as he was old enough to leave the house on his own, Zoan would have begun to learn his way about the streets of Caravaggio. Some of the town's tiny lanes ended in small courtyards; others opened suddenly into piazzas where capacious arcaded and roofed walkways joined one building to the next. There a little boy could take shelter from the scorching sun in summer or the pelting rain in winter under the cover of elegant Renaissance arches (in the newest buildings) or sturdy low ones (on the ground floor of its narrow-windowed medieval buildings).

Functionally happenstance is the most accurate description of the layout of Caravaggio's streets, lanes, alleys, and small piazzas. In the town's center two piazzas are now and were then connected to one another by a narrow street. One was devoted to commerce, the other dedicated to religion. From these two open spaces the city had grown outward, until it crammed five or six thousand people within its walls during Zoan's boyhood years and was the most populous town in the district, after Bergamo.[8]

Friday was market day, and then young Zoan would have run about among the stalls in the portico of the massive medieval Palazzo del Comune. Industries both large and small flourished in Caravaggio. Small merchants and craftsmen streamed into town through its several gates, some from as far away as Crema. Caravaggio's own silversmiths, carpenters, and coachmakers could hope to make sales as well (Santagiuliana 1981, 116).

Zoan would have known something of Caravaggio's history and of the heroic exploits of Giacomo, son of Antonio Secco. Born in 1465, his parents had been Antonio Secco, governor of Cremona, and Caterina Dal Verme, countess of Sangiunetto. Largely because of Giacomo's military leadership, Caravaggio had been miraculously spared the looting, rapine, and destruction that invading French forces had visited on outlying districts. Within the walls, however, common people believed Caravaggio's survival was yet another instance of the Virgin's special favor for their town (Secco d'Aragona 1968, 197–98).

The details of Straparola's story about Zambò of Valsabbia (night 5, story 3) suggest that as a boy Zoan had learned to prune winegrape vines. In his youth those would have been the barzamina grape that produced a locally consumed sweet and aromatic wine listed on tax rolls at the beginning of the 1500s (Santagiuliana 1981, 114). Grapevine pruning would turn out to be Zoan-as-Zambò's only bankable skill when he set out into the world beyond Caravaggio.[9]

Zoan's nickname Straparola bespeaks his most notable, even remarkable personal characteristic. As he grew up playing on the streets of Caravaggio, he probably had something to say about everything that happened and everybody who passed by. His parents couldn't shut him up. He interrupted his father. He added to what his mother had to say. He contradicted his brothers. And he couldn't stop talking in school, where his teacher, Signor Ravizza (see below), shushed him in vain.

That Zoan went to school is certain. As Paul Grendler's comprehensive history *Schooling in Renaissance Italy* (1989) demonstrates, there were intense efforts to educate urban boys in Renaissance Italy. Caravaggio with its four schools, one for the children of its noble and wealthy families and three for the rest of the town's young population (Santagiuliana 1981, 100), was perfectly in line with Renaissance practice. Signor Giovanni David de Aresi, "artis grammaticae professor," had long taught Caravaggio's young. When he left, Caravaggio's children spent long months without a schoolmaster, until the commune hired Giovita Ravizza in 1492. By that date, Zoan would have been sitting, or standing, in one of Caravaggio's communal schools.

The communal schools of northern Italy had a stable and relatively uninterrupted existence between 1300 and 1600, their teaching augmented by freelance schoolmasters. Although cathedral schools existed in some north Italian towns and cities, such as Pistoia, Verona, Venice, and Treviso, parish schools were uncommon, and so we should certainly imagine young Zoan in a communal rather than a church school.

The kind of schooling Zoan Francesco got was probably very like that available in Palazzolo sull'Oglio, a small town of twelve or thirteen hundred souls that lay midway between Brescia and Bergamo, only 13 or 14 miles (22 kilometers) from Caravaggio. As Grendler describes it, Palazzolo sull'Oglio had a communal school, which like many others in northern Italy hired a schoolmaster to teach two principal subjects. In the "abbaco schools" the first subject consisted of standard courses in commercial mathematics; the second was standard (Florentine) Italian. Texts commonly used in communal and vernacular schools included the *Fior di virtù*, with short chapters devoted to vivid stories of virtue and vice; the *Epistole e Evangeli che si leggono tutto l'anno alla messa*, that is, Old and New Testament liturgical scripture readings for the church year; *Le vite dei Santi Padri*, the lives of the church fathers or the *Legendario dei santi*, the collection of saints' lives known as the *Golden Legend*; and popular chivalric romances (Grendler 1995, 167). Latin was rarely part of the communal school curriculum, for it belonged to separate schools serving the wealthy. Both kinds of curricula were undoubtedly offered in Caravaggio, because Giovita Ravizza, Caravaggio's sole schoolmaster during the period in which young Zoan would have been attending a communal school, was a well-known humanist.

Education was not free, but recognizing, perhaps, that education fostered commerce, and that commerce increased both individual wealth and the common good, communes sometimes waived fees for poor but deserving pupils and forbade teachers from exacting additional fees. As Grendler observed about vernacular schools, "even conservative educational theorists endorsed education for boys of humble birth" (102), with the result that "The boy who went to school for a sufficient period of time could read chivalric romances, racy novelle, and exotic travel literature" (104). Teaching in Caravaggio's schools was apparently effective, because several of its youngsters grew up to become learned members of university faculties in northern Italy (Santagiuliana 1981, 120–25).

Experience in Caravaggio's building trades was equally effective in preparing young people for a professional life outside Caravaggio: Giovanni Mangone di Francesco made a name for himself as an architect in Rome. Eusebio da Caravaggio also went to Rome, as did Polidoro Caldara da Caravaggio in Lombardia, the geographically specific name given to him by Giorgio Vasari, the chronicler of Renaissance artists (Santagiuliana 1981, 102–3, 119–22).

One contemporary of Straparola's, Sabba Castiglione (1480–1554), recommended that girls, too, read Italy's classic authors, Dante, Petrarch, and Boccaccio, though not all their works. Not Dante's *Vita Nova*, not Petrarch's sonnets and songs, and not Boccaccio's *Decameron, Fiammetta*, or *Filocolo*. Girls—in advice familiar from later centuries all over Europe—should read religious works. Learning for girls might be dangerous, for it could lead to a career not anticipated by modern readers, that of courtesan, one of whose advertised charms was broad learning. One of Straparola's own heroines, Violante in "The Tailor's Apprentice" (night 8, story 4), bears the name given to a portrait by Titian of one of Venice's most beautiful courtesans. With her bleached hair, an alluring color many Venetian courtesans adopted, with her bosom immodestly displayed in an inviting dishabille utterly alien to portraits of merchant wives and aristocratic women, Titian's Violante bespeaks sexual availability. As long as such well-schooled girls retained the freshness and beauty of youth, they could mix with the upper levels of male Venetian society. Straparola's naming the heroine of "The Tailor's Apprentice" "Violante," which could hardly have been lost on contemporary readers, fit perfectly with the social and sexual ambiguity that existed in Straparola's assemblage of fictive female narrators in the frametale he created to surround his stories. (See Chapter 4 for further discussion of the sexual ambiguities of Straparola's female frametale narrators.)

If Straparola's life began as humbly as I suspect, it meant schooling in the vernacular rather than in Latin. That fact alone would have excluded him from employment that required a thorough grounding in the classics. Such limited examples of Latin as exist in his writing are insufficient to support claims like Simona Rizzardi's that he had mastered that language (Rizzardi 1989 63).[10] If Zoan Straparola had not learned Latin as a boy, he could have done so as an adult, as did Piero della Francesca (Grendler 1995, 168–70). And for writers whose Latin was faulty, Venice had plenty of well-schooled editors who could fix mistakes. Until there is more evidence of Straparola's writing in Latin, the extent of his knowledge of that ancient tongue must be left an open question.

Zoan's early years in Caravaggio would not have been all pruning vines and adding sums. Outside the city gates south of town, the church of San Bernardino da Siena was abuilding and was giving work and experience to large numbers of skilled artisans and casual laborers. Drawn by workplace activity, young Zoan might have watched, helped, or even worked.

Another church, the Sanctuary of the Blessed Virgin of Caravaggio (Sanctuario della Beata Vergine da Caravaggio), still a simple wooden structure in the late 1400s and early 1500s, attracted hundreds of pilgrims. The church commemorated the Virgin's appearance to a poor young peasant woman, Giovanetta Vachi, on May 26, 1432. Brutally beaten by her drunken husband Francesco Varoli, she had prayed to the Virgin so fervently that May afternoon that Mary had appeared. Physical proof of her account were the miraculous springs gushing forth at the spot where Giovanetta said that the Virgin's foot had touched the earth.

The world, or at least the part of the world that sought a miraculous cure at Caravaggio's sanctuary, passed by the town's children and adults like a moving spectacle. Gilt and painted sedan chairs carried tender women whose city-bred feet could not suffer Caravaggio's rough paving stones. Men of means, flashy and arrogant, held the reins in child-crushingly heavy two-wheeled *carrozze* and maneuvered dangerously along the crowded cobbled streets. Some wore the opulent velvets and satins of the wealthy. Others were poor, and looked like poor people everywhere, in dun-dull dusty clothes, sagging socks, frayed sandals, their skirts or trousers held up with belts of ill-matching cloth, leather, or rope.

The End of Childhood

Zoan's childhood came to a sudden end in the early 1500s. Paul Larivaille saw Straparola's childhood and adolescent biography in Costantino Fortunato's life history (night 11, story 1): happy poverty fractured by a mother's death and followed by an unequal distribution of family goods to Zoan and his brothers (1973, 65). Larivaille, who adopted Marc Soriano's interpretation of the youngest son as "féminöide" but aspiring to dominance and virility, believed that the psychic state evident in the story of Costantino and his cat was a projection of Straparola's own psyche, and that he himself had been too soon abandoned by a mother's death and had been exposed to expropriation by coarse brothers. To confirm his understanding of Straparola's youth, Larivaille hoped that someone would eventually provide a psycho-critical treatment of Straparola's oeuvre (65).

Something of a psychocritical treatment of Straparola's collection of tales underlies the following analysis, for his prose provides important clues about a psychological calamity that took place during his youth It was not, however, the calamitous event found in the tale of Costantino Fortunato (night 11, story 1), but in the tale of Fortunio (night 3, story 4). Fortunio's identification with Straparola himself is supported by the story's geographical location of the hero's childhood— in the most distant (*estreme*) parts of Lombardy, which from the vantage point of Venice described Caravaggio's position exactly.

The household in which Zoan grew up was probably as stable as the average Caravaggio household. Zoan's parents were probably married and would have lived together for some years before Zoan entered their lives. If we take the story of Fortunio as emblematically autobiographical, we can imagine Straparola's mother as worthy and amiable, the father as not well off, but possessing good qualities of head and heart, as the story stated:

There was, then, in the far parts of Lombardy, a man named Bernio, who whatever abundant goods fate had not bestowed on him, was held to be in his spirit and heart not inferior to others. He took for his wife a worthy and kind lady named Alchia, who though socially low, was endowed with ability and praiseworthy habits, and who loved her husband as much as any other woman who could be found.

Bernio and Alchia, long childless, sought a baby at that place where parents abandoned their children and found one "who was prettier and more charming than the others" *(più bello e più vezzoso de gli altri)*. We may imagine that Straparola's own adoptive parents had done the same thing. At some point after taking Fortunio into their household, Alchia became pregnant and bore her own and Bernio's child, Valentino. Fortunio did not know that he had been adopted until Valentino one day called him a bastard born of a wicked woman *(bastardo e nato di vil femina)*.

In no other story did Straparola write with such deep feeling as he did about the devastating effect this sudden knowledge had on Fortunio. The sharpness of his pain and the physiological exactness with which Straparola described it bespeak a keenly felt personal experience: "dagger-thrusts in his heart" and "sorrow upon sorrow" *(coltellate al cuore ... doglia sopra doglia)* tightened his throat. At last, with his unending grief and his suffering heart about to drive him to suicide (in a phrase borrowed from Boccaccio; Pirovano 2000, 218n5), Fortunio determined to flee Bernio's house and seek his fortune elsewhere.

Personal grief was not the only reason that might have pushed Zoan-as-Fortunio away from Caravaggio. In Zoan's childhood and youth Caravaggio had remained a relatively peaceful place of steady church-building, busy market days, and profitable pilgrims' visits. There was little internal impetus to leave. Political and economic conditions changed abruptly, however, with the arrival of the French king Louis XII and his armies on the Lombard plains in 1499. His appearance inaugurated thirty years of uncertainty and siege, pestilence and famine. Once again Caravaggio and the countryside around it passed back and forth between the jurisdiction and rule of the republic of Venice and the duchy of Milan, while on the local level the city was handed from one overlord to another. As the warring continued year after year, the Holy Roman Emperor Charles V and the next king of France, Francis I, brought their military forces over the Alps into northern Italy to contend for power and territory, and the inhabitants of Caravaggio were subjected to hunger and humiliation. In 1499 the distant city of Venice added insult to injury: it required Caravaggio to build at its own expense a soaring tower adjoining the church of Saints Fermo and Rustico as a visual demonstration of Venetian power (Scaperrota 2000, sheet 2).

Caravaggio had now become a place to flee. Little boys playing in its streets would have known that, if they were to make their fortunes, as Fortunio was determined to do, it would not be in Caravaggio but in the great world beyond, in cities like Milan, Mantua, or Verona, or further afield, in Messina, as Polidoro Caldara had done, or in Florence, Rome, Naples, Ferrara, or Venice, where many other Caravaggians had sought and sometimes found their fortune. Those cities had wealthy noble families or, in the case of Venice, the wealth of a prosperous republic. Such places meant money being spent, money that could be earned.

Large numbers of Caravaggio's young people left in the early years of the 1500s (Anon. 1991, 7–8, 30–31; Santagiuliana 1981, 83–132). For instance, Polidoro Caldara left Caravaggio to seek his fortune in Rome, where work was to be had because the papacy was still engaged in the monumental constructions that all Catholic Europe was financing. There Raphael was at work on his great paintings and frescos in the papal palace and Michelangelo's designs for Saint Peter's were beginning to take shape. Young Polidoro, who had probably gotten his first experience in the building of Caravaggio's San Bernardino da Siena, was initially a humble mortar-carrier, but his talent for drawing and painting eventually made his fortune, and he later executed commissions in Rome, Naples, and Messina. Polidoro's emigration to Rome typified the routes chosen by Caravaggio youth. Artisans skilled in all sorts of trades—carpenters, workers in intaglio and ebony, coachmakers, silversmiths, tinsmiths, "architetti," knife makers, swordsmiths—left town in those years. The emigration had complex roots, but basically expressed a common desire to move from limited economic opportunities in Caravaggio to expanding opportunities in Rome, Venice, and other cities. Emigration was given a further, and powerful, impulse by the threat of military incursion at home (Santagiuliana 1981, 118).

If Zoan's schooling had given him a taste of a life of words, of play with words and creating stories from them, then it would also have created in him a taste for a literary life, a life of the mind, of borrowing other people's stories and putting them into his own words. That life could not be lived in the small economy of Caravaggio, but it might be a possibility in the great city of Venice.

From Caravaggio to Venice

Let us accept the 1480s date of birth that reference books assign to Straparola and let us further assume that he left home when his beard began to sprout, the age at which parents had long sent their sons abroad to learn the life of trade and to become acquainted with foreign customs. Zoan would have left Caravaggio just as the adopted Fortunio had done. His route, however, could not have been described by Fortunio's magical passage through wild and desert locations and his encounters with speaking animals. Instead, Zoan Straparola would have gone east to Venice as did the hero of another tale, Zambò.

Straparola's distant goal was the capital city of the republic of Venice, a mercantile entrepôt rich beyond provincial imaginings, an international seaport with swaggering sailors, a sea power whose massive shipbuilding capacity supplied the defense of its maritime trading empire. Venice was also the Italian center of printing, introduced less than fifty years before from the north, a city that during Straparola's lifetime produced more books than the rest of Italy together. The printing trades employed large numbers of men from Brescia, a town on the way from Caravaggio to Venice. As typesetters and copyeditors, Brescians formed the backbone of the printing trade. Venice was, in short, a place where Zoan's exuberant native tongue might help him realize an adolescent vision of wealth beyond measure.

The "myth of Venice"—its reputation for beauty and liberty, peacefulness and republicanism (Muir 1981, 25–28)—was accepted by foreigners and repeated by natives. In the late 1400s and early 1500s the myth was strong and would grow stronger with each succeeding decade. Visitors then and later "lauded Venice as incomparably beautiful to see, marvelous to contemplate, secure, peaceful, and rich . . . after Paradise, Venice was the best place in the universe . . . [Venice was] a seaborne Venus" (Muir 1981, 14–15). Such a reputation must have pulled Zoan toward Venice as much as military conflict and personal grief pushed him out of Caravaggio.

In traveling toward Venice, Zoan probably walked (Demnati 1989, 13). In his part of the country that was how the physically able poor got from one place to another. He could have taken either of two routes that linked Caravaggio to Venice. One led south from Caravaggio, eventually merging with old, flat, straight Roman road beds and passing through the broad Po Valley from Crema, Cremona, Mantua, and Padua to Venice. This route, however, crossed the political borders of the duchies of Milan and Mantua before reentering the safe domain of the Venetian republic.

The other route began at Caravaggio's gate in the eastern wall of the city, crossed the stony-bedded Serio and Oglio Rivers, and passed through Rovato, Brescia, Verona, Vicenza, and Padua before arriving in Venice. This was a pleasantly hilly route, with the advantage that no political borders had to be passed. The great likelihood is that Zoan opted for the hillier but more certain northern route.

It was not easy for Zoan to leave his native town. Caravaggio had suckled him, had reared him, had educated him, had raised him from a street-silly boy to a capable young man. He carried its image within him and he published heartfelt sentiments about his birthplace at the 1508 conclusion of his *New Works*:

Sonnet 114 O Caravaggio

O Caravaggio, blessed citadel
How fortunate you now are
Enjoying my lord Giacomo full of joy
Who maintains you by his so exalted virtue.

As if to confer honor [he was] born to the world
One feels his glory moving all about
Bringing good fortune in every place, although
It cannot be spoken of enough: desired by everyone.

In him reigns the Secco flower of every virtue,
The muses celebrate him:
He who is a magnificent glory of all knowledge.

He is courageous in speech, humble in appearance,
Sweet in his smile, full of love in his heart
In sum, he is a treasure and fountain of all wisdom.[11]

We can observe young Zoan trying out a courtier's skills, flattering Giacomo Secco, who now headed the Caravaggio family, punning on his name, even playfully aligning himself with the name of this ancient land-wealthy family (*seco* was Straparola's spelling of Secco—with oneself). But Straparola's literarily crafted references are infused with an evident psychological and social distance: he addressed Caravaggio familiarly in the second person, Giacomo only in the third person.[12] Straparola was obviously trying to secure patronage from "Iacomo,"[13] but it is unlikely that he succeeded. Giacomo was far too busy looking for patronage for himself in Mantua, Ferrara, and Milan to think of conferring it on an unknown son of Caravaggio twenty years his junior.

Zoan's beloved Caravaggio grew smaller in the distance as he strode eastward toward Rovato and on toward Venice. Perhaps he, like

Costantino Fortunato, bore the disfiguring marks of poverty on his face and body. He was a poor boy, and he needed to work to earn his bread on the long walk. Perhaps he found the kinds of jobs in the towns through which he passed that were common in labor-intensive daily life in the 1500s. He might, for example, have financed his meals by carrying goods on his shoulders from one town to the next. To tell the story of this long journey, Straparola reverted to dialect and borrowed another, and well-known, tale and put it into the mouth of the frametale narrator Antonio Molino who had in real life published a comic piece in Bergamesque dialect that included a Bergamo laborer (Pirovano 2000, 1: 357n1). Then he filled out the plot with detailed testimony of "Zambò"'s trip to Venice from the town of Valsabbia, 24 miles (40 km) northeast of Brescia. There is such a persuasively pressing reality about the sequence of events that we may be excused for understanding it as a personal reminiscence. The story was filled with sharply etched, memorable (and probably remembered) details such as shoes of red pigskin, a master cap-maker, and above all, the hero's ingenuous and unworldly truth-telling. In addition, it is one of the *Pleasant Nights*'s two tales told in dialect, in this case, the Bergamo dialect that Zoan would have known from his childhood. Straparola set the story (night 5, story 3) in a year of great scarcity and famine, during which Zambò

filled a pouch with some bread and cheese and a little bottle of wine, put on a pair of red pigskin shoes, left home and went towards Brescia. But not finding any [way to earn money], he went to Verona, where he found a master cap-maker, who asked him if he knew how to make caps, to which he answered no; and seeing that there was nothing for him there, he left Verona, and Vicenza, and came to Padua; and having seen that there were certain doctors (*medegh*), who asked him whether he knew how to drive mules, he answered no, but that he could till the land and tend vines; and not being able to reach any agreement with them, he left there to go to Venice.

Zambò's earnestly truthful reply to the doctors that he knew only how to till the soil and tend vines seems to embed an essential psychological truth that may well bear a message about Straparola himself. Four hundred and fifty years after the fact, the hero's shooting-himself-in-the-foot answer suggests that fragments of Zoan Francesco Straparola's own boyhood character, hints of personal adolescent experience, and indications of a disarmingly attractive openness lie embedded in the fictive persona that inhabits the early parts of the Zambò story.

The rest of the novella's plot can be found in numerous earlier

collections of tales—Doni's *Novelle*, *The Seven Sages of Rome*, and Sercambi's *Novelle*. In the form that Straparola gave the story, the protagonist subsequently became a vicious and ugly dissembler who expropriated
his wife's goods, beat her black and blue, and was repaid in kind by
being murdered and disposed of in the Tiber. There is both psychological disjunction and narrative friction between the beginning and the
conclusion of the story; Straparola had apparently seized the occasion to
insert his life as young Zambò into his own collection as he neared the
end of Book 1.[14]

Venice in the Early 1500s

Zambò's story, if we believe it to be in part autobiographical, gets Zoan
Straparola to Venice. In the late 1490s and early 1500s Venice was a
city of civic spectacles finely detailed in Gentile Bellini's paintings. It
was also the city of Vittore Carpaccio's meticulously delineated public
gatherings and domestic furnishings, Giovanni Bellini's stunning secular
portraits, religious moments, and mythological scenes, and Giorgione's
gloriously coloristic paintings. On any one of Venice's many days of
civic celebration, young Zoan Straparola could have walked among
the individuals recorded a few years earlier in Carpaccio's 1494 painting *The Healing of the Possessed Man*. Gondolas jostle each other on
the water, pedestrians pass shoulder to shoulder on the Rialto bridge,
and officials and observers press closely together in and on the edge of
the water of the canal. Some dress sumptuously, others plainly, while
chimney pots punctuating the city skyline and laundry hanging out
to dry testify to unseen interiors with their domestic hearths and
washbasins.[15]

In his first weeks and months in Venice, Straparola probably experienced the city's gritty side. Once again Zambò's story (night 5, story 3)
provides likely details:

Zambò wandered around the city for a long time, and not having found work
and not having a penny so that he could eat, he was in a bad way. But after a
long time, when he was in God's grace, he came to Fusina,[16] and because he was
penniless nobody would take any interest in him, so that the poor man didn't
know what to do. And seeing that the boatmen who turned the machines for
drawing boats ashore earned a few farthings, he set himself to doing such work.
But fate, which always persecutes the poor, the slackers, and the disgraced,

arranged that one day when he was turning the machine, the leather strap snapped, unwound, and made a spar hit him in the chest and that threw him to the ground unconscious, where for a time he lay stretched out like a corpse and if certain kind-hearted men hadn't hauled him into their boat by his arms and legs and rowed him back to Venice, he would have died there.

The prose is flawed, for it shows Zambò both felled to the *ground* and being pulled from the *water*. Nonetheless, the emotionally laden and factually detailed description of his workplace injury feels so real that we may impute the crash of a heavy wooden spar onto Zambò's unprotected chest to painful personal experience.

Straparola placed this event in Fusina, a common point of embarkation from the mainland for Venice, but it could just as well have taken place in the Arsenal at the eastern end of the city. During Straparola's lifetime there was an immense galley presence in Venice with consequent and concurrent shipbuilding, among whose transient workforce were sawyers from the province of Bergamo (Davis 1991, 108). The Arsenal was one place where every ablebodied person, male or female,

Figure 1. "La Ville de Venise," from *Epitome de la corographie d'Europe*, trans. Guillaume Gueroult (Lyons: Balthazar Armoullet, 1553), 37. Typ 515 53.439 F, Department of Printing and Graphic Arts, Houghton Library, Harvard College Library.

could always find employment (Lane 1965, 219–32). If Straparola's narrative accident took place in Fusina, therefore, it is probably because it *did* take place there, insistently but awkwardly inserting itself into the story.

Finally finding work he knew how to do, Zambò began working for an herbalist named Vivia Vianel from Chiozza, whose vines he tended and for whom he performed errands. The next passage in Zambò's Venetian adventures incorporated the joyous wordplay that gave Straparola his descriptive cognomen. The story's repartee reflected not the quick-but-imperfect response of the streets, but the often rehearsed and perfectly phrased ripostes of a well-prepared anecdote: having eaten two of the three figs he was to have delivered to Vianel's friend, Ser Peder, Zambò announced his transgression. Ser Peder asked how he could have done such a thing, to which Zambò impudently replied, "Like this," and brazenly ate the third!

The Zambò plot's sequence of set pieces show the fictional hero passing from physical labor to literary wordplay. If the experiences of the fictional Zambò may stand for those of the young Straparola, then we may also construe the title of his *New Works . . . Recently Published* (1508) as a hint that it contained additions to already existing works. Even though *New Works* was a fairly common title for collections of verse and prose in Straparola's day, may we not posit now-lost "old works" that he had published, or presented, before 1508? Or old works that he had incorporated into his volume entitled *New Works?* One example might be "O Caravaggio" itself, if, for example, he had offered it to Giacomo Secco at an earlier point. Furthermore, if Straparola had found work as a hired pen at any time in the past, that work would be consistent with his having published, or having presented, single verses before 1508 as samples of his skill with words—in other words, other forms of "Old Works."

Zoan's journey to Venice forms no part of any story other than that of Zambò. Bergamo itself surfaced only once, in his tale of Bergamesque trickery to confound visiting Florentines (night 9, story 5). Caravaggio, for its part, appears in the *Pleasant Nights* only on the book's title page as part of his own name, although a place that could have been Caravaggio, as noted earlier, appeared as a town in the furthest reaches of Lombardy in the tale of Fortunio, whose plot and style suggest biographical details. For the most part, Straparola separated his former life in the provincial hinterlands from his new life in the Venetian capital.

If we want to see what a young man of modest means looked like in the years in which Straparola published his *New Works*, we can inspect Lorenzo Lotto's portrait of a *Young Man Against a White Curtain*, painted in 1508, the same year that Zoan launched his publishing career (Figure 2). With a serious but uncertain expression and an unsmiling mouth, the brown-haired youth looks toward the painter facing him

Figure 2. Lorenzo Lotto, *Young Man Against a White Curtain* (ca. 1508). Reproduced by permission of Bildarchiv, Kunsthistorisches Museum, Vienna.

with a pained expression. This is most certainly *not* Zoan Straparola, who at this point in his life would not have scowled at the observing world, but would have sought favor with an ingratiating "play of the eyes that shall give an effect of grace," as Castiglione had described the ideal courtier (Castiglione, 45). Instead, here sits a young man of high social status, whose uncomfortable aspect verges on arrogance. What is interesting in this context is the plain dark clothing and the brown color and the shoulder length of the young man's hair, so typical of Venetian portraits in the early 1500s, all of which help us imagine Zoan Straparola's appearance as a young man seeking his fortune in Venice in the early years of the sixteenth century.

Between physical labor and a literary career lies a space of time in which we can surmise little about Straparola's life, unless, like Zambò, he too married a widow with a shop. That however, is unlikely, and so let us return to Venice herself, the Queen of the Adriatic, to understand the world in which Zoan Straparola moved about on a daily basis.

The year in Venice began on March 1 with a fifteen-day spring fair that inaugurated the theater season, which then continued through the spring into midsummer (Muir 1981, 120–21). The celebration of Corpus Christi was mounted in early summer, with a magnificent procession that incorporated elaborate floats with tableaux vivants of Old Testament stories and of the church fathers (Pullan 1971, 38ff.; Muir 1981, 225–27). The floats were built by various *Scuole*, formal social organizations originally founded for rigorously religious practice but which in the early sixteenth century had become providers of charitable relief for needy members. In October 1511, for instance, the *Scuola della Miseracordia* headed the annual procession, with "twenty-seven little boys dressed like small angels, all carrying vessels of silver in their hands, while others bore the arms of the League, the pope, the King of Spain, the King of England, and of St. Mark and of [the Venetian] Signoria." Each time Venice joined a political alliance against the French invaders—as it did in 1511, 1513, 1526, and 1530—the city's government marked the occasion with similarly vivid public displays (Pullan 1971, 53).

The calendar year ended with the public entertainments of Carneval, which began on the day after Christmas and lasted until the beginning of Lent more than a month later. Edward Muir's *Civic Ritual in Renaissance Venice* (1981) documents the staggering array of entertainments put on for public amusement: bull chases, human pyramids, comedies, fireworks, feasts, masquerades, and fighting. Until 1525, when the Venetian government tried to reform the festivities, the city staged a comic burlesque of its own practices by condemning a bull and twelve pigs to death, allowing them to be chased through the streets, and decapitating them in front of the Ducal Palace (Muir 1981, 156, 161). When national merchant companies sponsored outlandish spectacles, like that of the Germans on Fat Tuesday in 1517, they produced "jousts, bull chases, battles between dogs and a bear, a transvestite ballet, and an allegorical pageant. These were not performances arranged by amateurs, but by specialist entertainers like the quick-change artist Zuan Polo in the 1510s and the entertainment designer of mock battles and jousts Zuan Cosaza" (Muir 1981, 166–67). Sometimes a theme, such as regeneration or the battle between the sexes, dominated the festivities, and then, with ribaldry the common coin, there were exhibits like Priapus with a gigantic phallus (Muir 1981, 173–74). It was just such vulgar entertainments that unfolded noisily across the waters from the fictive storytelling gathering on the island of Murano in the *Pleasant Nights*.

Even administering justice formed part of the year's entertainments, as repellent as it might seem to the contemporary reader. In the Piazzetta citizens could gape at condemned felons wearing crowns decorated with devils. Lower-class criminals, convicted of relatively minor crimes against the state or of heinous ones against individuals, were publicly mutilated and put to death equally publicly (Muir 1981, 246). In a highly ritualized execution, one serial rapist who had attacked more than eighty women was dragged by a horse from Santa Croce to San Marco, beheaded and quartered, his four body parts hung on the scaffold itself ("Diary of Marino Sanuto," 1 August 1513 in Chambers and Pullan 1992, 89–90). Upper-class criminals were delivered from this life with slightly more speed and humanity. Although only one or two civically sponsored executions like these took place per year, each execution's oozing blood, dangling body parts, and general gore must have brutalized public consciousness.[17]

In the early 1500s Venice, called "La Serenissima," was a city that seemed to be at the height of her power. Her government, a republican form with rotating patrician officeholders under a doge elected for life, promoted commerce and had been remarkably stable for centuries. From a long history of seaborne trade abroad and of international marketing at home she was fabulously rich. Books, jewels, glass, carpets, carnelian beads for a rosary—everything was available, with the highest prices "on the Riva" and lower ones in other parts of the city, as

Albrecht Dürer wrote to friends who had asked him to shop for them in Venice (Dürer 1913, 3, 8–15, 17, 20, 23)!

Commerce meant large numbers of merchants from the Italian peninsula, from beyond the Adriatic, and from the other side of the Alps and the Dolomites. It meant even larger numbers of sailors from the furthest shores of the Mediterranean world. In the 1500s Venice's republican stability itself rested on a foundation of economically enduring family structures achieved by wealthy families who by custom dowered one or more daughters for an advantageous marriage alliance while consigning the rest to convents and who allowed one son to marry in order to carry on the family line while depriving other sons of the right to establish legitimate families that would, if allowed to come into existence, diminish the core family's wealth (Davis 1975 passim; Chojnacki 1994, 93–106). These two factors, a flourishing commercial economy and a limiting marriage policy among noble families, created an enormous appetite for sexual services.

That appetite was supplied in part by cloistered daughters themselves. Some Venetian noblewomen had fallen from their formerly chaste conduct (Gilbert 1973, 275), nor was this anything new (Ruggiero 1985, 70–88). In Straparola's day many daughters whose noble fathers wished not to dower them sufficiently for marriage were placed in the convents of Santa Maria delle Vergini, where they lived a secular life and received admirers and lovers. The same was true of the convent of San Zaccaria. Scandalized, city fathers instituted forcible reforms, but just a few years later, several "nuns'" maidservants were found to be bawds. Illicit visits and secret liaisons continued, because the nuns, most of whom were noblewomen, had highly placed fathers, uncles, and brothers who protected them: "their fathers cannot marry them to their equals because they are not rich enough to do so, and will not marry them to lesser men for fear of tarnishing the prestige of their families." So wrote Alberto Bolognetti in 1580, describing conditions of long duration (Chambers and Pullan 1992, 208).

Such noble girls and women would likely have taken only men of high rank as lovers. For the rest of Venice's unattached noble sons and for its merchants and sailors, Venice had immense numbers of prostitutes. In 1500, for a population of 100,000, there were 12,000 prostitutes (Davis 1975, 105), 11,654 to be exact (Rosenthal 1992, 11). Defined legally in a Senate decree of 1543, prostitutes were "those women who, being unmarried, have dealings and intercourse with one man or more [and also] those who have husbands and do not live with them, but are separated from them and have dealings with one man or more" (Senate decree of 21 February 1542, in Chambers and Pullan 1992, 127). The proportion of Venice's population engaged in the sex trade remained similarly high during Straparola's entire lifetime. Prostitutes were so integral a part of Venetian life that the republic had made humane provisions for their protection as early as 1460 (Collegio regulations in Chambers and Pullan 1992, 120–23).

Some men, especially among the upper classes, preferred male sexual partners. In the disapproving words of a contemporary, "Young Venetian nobles and citizens tricked themselves out with so many ornaments, and with garments that opened to show the chest, and with so many perfumes, that there was no indecency in the world to compare with the frippery and finery of Venetian youth and their provocative acts of luxury and venery" (Priuli 1509, in Chambers and Pullan 1992, 124). In 1511 the patriarch of Venice claimed that "the female whores . . . say that they cannot make a living because no one now goes to them, so rampant is sodomy" (Diary of Marino Sanuto, 27 March 1511, in Chambers and Pullan 1992, 189). In response, some female prostitutes adopted men's hairstyles to service homosexual men, that is, "to please men by pretending to be men" (Decree of the Council of Ten, 1480, in Chambers and Pullan 1992, 123; Ruggiero 1985, 119–20). This was the Venice immediately before Zoan Straparola's eyes, the Venice in which he lived and where he tried to make a living.

A different Venetian history was unfolding across the waters that separated Venice from the mainland to the west and north and from the Mediterranean to the southeast. Maritime trade, which had filled many Venetian coffers, had always involved unpredictable risk from wind, waves, and piracy. In the 1500s the Portuguese were emerging as serious competitors for the Far Eastern trade in spices. In such a financial climate, the mainland became for Venetian nobles, merchants, and shopkeepers an increasingly attractive location for investment and for second homes (Gullino 1994). "Italy" didn't exist as a political entity and mainland expansion on Venice's part meant antagonizing powers on both sides of the Alps who had interests in and on the Italian peninsula. Consequently, Venice's expansion on the mainland met a formidable military response. In 1508, France, Spain, the Holy Roman Empire, and the Papacy together with various Italian states formed an alliance against Venice, the League of Cambrai, and their overwhelming strength routed the Venetian army at the Battle of Agnadello on May 14, 1509. Although allegiances within the League shifted quickly and dramatically, depredations, lootings, and burnings continued for years in northern Italy.

Zoan Straparola's position in the city was uncertain at best. He didn't have, and probably never would have, the privileges and perquisites that belonged hereditarily to that 4–5 percent of the population that constituted Venice's nobility. Neither was he a *cittadino*, one of the 5 percent who made up a "lower-level hereditary elite [who could aspire to] careers in the permanent civil service, the lower echelons of the diplomatic corps, the law, notarial offices, trade, and medicine" (Muir 1981, 38). The legal status of *cittadino* was reserved for people who had been born in Venice and who had not engaged in manual labor for three generations—not a requirement Straparola could meet.

Straparola would have remained one of the *popolani*, who comprised the mass of Venetian population and embraced social groups as disparate as manual laborers, artisans, and merchants, some of them very wealthy. In terms of literacy, most manual laborers probably couldn't read, but urban apprentices and artisans typically could, and merchants certainly could.[18] In the 1500s the same people were experiencing, and suffering from, a "growing divergence between the classes" (Muir 1981, 42). That meant that Zoan had to scramble to make a living as one among many boys of thirteen, fourteen, and fifteen on their own learning the ropes in Venice (Tucci 1973, 364–65). As an immigrant from a town near Bergamo, he may also have shared the ridicule reserved for newcomers from Bergamo and the surrounding province.

Under these circumstances, it is reasonable to assume that Straparola would have protested his differentness. *He* came from the rich Lombard plain, not from the hardscrabble valleys atop which Bergamo perched. Nonetheless, he would have spoken, at least when he first arrived, in accents that identified him as one of those insignificant Bergamesques who traditionally worked as servants, porters, and ferrymen in Venice (Demnati 1989, 13). If we accept Zambò's portside injury as Straparola's own experience, then after it he would no longer have been fit for the hard physical exertion those jobs entailed (although the less rigorous vinedressing remained a possibility).

What might have been Straparola's condition in the years between 1508 and 1515? Probably in his twenties, and—if we accept Zambò's arrival in Venice as Zoan's—with a damaged constitution, but able to display freshly published proof of his way with words, he would have been an excellent candidate for personal service. Patricians were routinely burdened with responsibilities that ranged from civic governance to family investments and included personal interests. The early 1500s was a period when "a small group of men was desperately struggling with an endless number of unexpected and diverse tasks" (Gilbert 1973, 281). In short, it was a perfect time for a man of letters to seek a position with an overburdened official. Then, as now, an overcommitted man of affairs needed a trusted and literate secretary to extend his capacities. Could Zoan have performed those tasks day by day in some small chamber in a still unidentified Venetian Ca', stifling his penchant for talk?

Other possibilities also existed, at least in theory, though we may never know definitively about Straparola's life between 1508 and 1515. Was he offered a position as a scrivener of the republic? Was he hired by a municipality on the mainland or in Venice to teach in a communal school? Did a group of parents hire him collectively to tutor their young? Any of these is as possible as serving in a noble household between 1508 and 1515. Overall, Straparola's asides in the *Pleasant Nights* testify to familiarity with comfortable domestic arrangements: he had watched women make meat pies at home (night 3, story 2), and he knew how servants used a large vessel to smooth out underclothes (night 4, story 1). It is entirely possible, therefore, that he first proved his ability in a government position and then became a household retainer with a noble family in Venice, which would have placed him on the social periphery of wealth and power.

None of the earning possibilities outlined here offered a personal social status of any significance. If Zoan Straparola were to raise his status, he would need to find a patron. He had added only two new sonnets to his *New Works* in the seven years between 1508 and 1515, which suggests that in those years he had not written under his own name, but that his writing had served other people's needs or even that he might have been ghostwriting for one or more wealthy but literarily untalented young men pursuing a literary life or amorous adventures. Perhaps he had done so for the "miser Lafranco" whom he named in the dedication of the 1508 edition. In 1515 Straparola renewed his search for a patron and republished his *New Works*. He probably succeeded, because no writings appeared under his own name for another thirty-five years.

Straparola's *Opera Nova*

Zoan published his little book in 1508. He gave it an unassuming title, *Opera nova de Zoan Francesco Straparola da Caravazo novamente stampata*. Title pages then, and for several centuries afterwards, both described and advertised the book of which they were a part. And so we must be impressed by Zoan's unusual modesty in simply listing its contents: 115 sonnets, 35 strambotti, 7 "epistre," and 12 "capitoli." The crudely executed woodcut title page illustration on the edition of 1515, with its three men and three women, advertised itself visually to a gender-mixed buyership.

The style and content of Straparola's 115 sonnets in the *Opera nova* make it abundantly evident that he, like so many Italian poets before and after him, took Petrarch as model and ideal. His Laura was "the most noble Madonna Helene," probably a woman as respectably married to someone else as Petrarch's Laura had been. Drawing on the glorious past, Zoan invoked a literary heritage that was ancient classical as well as Italian classic: Paris and Troy (Sonnet 7), Diana (passim), and Dante (Sonnet 5).

Straparola's Helene was beauteous in her forehead, nose, eyes, hand, and lips, but when he praised her teeth as well (Sonnet 12), he turned a high ideal into a mundane catalog. Like versifying lovers before him, Straparola-as-author suffered poetically in his "pecto" (breast) because of her "belleza" (beauty), "gentileza" (courtesy), and "bionda treza" (blond hair; Sonnet 40 and others).

Expressions of courtly love abounded. The literary form required the author's longing love, but the social form exacted unending frustration (Sonnet 54). Consequently, despite his lacerated heart (Sonnet 88) and death's call (Sonnets 92, 93), his beloved's heart remained virginal (Sonnet 105).

In the *Strambotti*, Straparola addressed the same subjects but in a more compact and lyrical form. With their "narrar," "gesti," and "parole" (recounting, gestures, words), the *Strambotti* intimated an oral rather than a book culture. The verses' images, however, continued a centuries' old literary tradition: he was in such torment (*in tal tormento*) and was repeatedly consumed in flames in the many years in which he had suffered (*tanti anni / ho sopportato sopra el lasto dorso / gionto*).

The rhymed *Epistolae*, also directed to "his mistress," advanced to a grammatically more intimate level (te, tuo, ti): "Signora mia, ho visto tua scritura piena damaritudine per certo" (Epistola 5). But by the seventh and last rhymed letter, Straparola returned to the more formal "your" of "vostro cor" (your heart). One wonders if Straparola had become stylistically careless or if he had been formally rebuffed.

The twelve *Capitoli* as a whole sustained Straparola's narrative of unrequited love. Filled with tears and sighs (*lachryme & sospiri*), its author declared in No. 8 that he couldn't live without his beloved (*io senza di te viver non posso*) and, despite his pure and youthful condition (*pura & giovenil estade*), he ended by intending to throw his body into a ditch.

"Cruel" had been a codeword for at least 300 years for a beloved who had not "healed" a lover who was dying for her "favor" by being "kind" to him. And so, in an afterword not listed on the title page, a melodramatic and "cruel" leavetaking from his mistress left the author with miserable pain but reassured the reader (and above all, his beloved's husband!) that the poet's passion had remained virtuously unrequited. Leaving his heart, his spirit, and his fidelity with his lady (*donna mia*), he predicted that his misery would end in his death.

What, beyond the unconvincing sentiments expressed there, can we read out of Straparola's *New Works ... Newly Printed*? He was a young man, as he said in the *Capitoli*. Like every young Italian who had been to school, he knew of Petrarch and could hardly have escaped being aware of the impressively rich worldly rewards that Petrarch's poetry (albeit *Latin* poetry) had won him—offers of employment from the pope, ambassadorships, the company of kings, a rich library that he had bequeathed to the city of Venice, and a comfortable retirement. Any ambitious young man would have wished for the same rewards for demonstrated talent, but Straparola's efforts achieved only a pre-Bembo Venetian Petrarchism, in the words of Manlio Pastore Stocchi (Straparola 1979, viii).

Chances are that Straparola's published verse, second rate though it was, found him a Venetian patron into whose service he put his pen. Not only did he have a demonstrated ability to produce verse, he could also provide amusing prose *facetiae* or enigmas with double meanings, and in those days such mastery of northern Italy's cultural patrimony would provide entry to high social circles, to judge from Castiglione's descriptions in *The Courtier*, especially in books 2 and 3.

Straparola and Patronage

Let us take a closer look at what it means to suggest that Straparola probably found a patron. Patronage in Venice, as Jennifer Fletcher has noted, "is generally difficult to document" (Chambers and Pullan 1992, 417). Nonetheless, Peter Burke, who examined the subject, found several examples of literary patronage in Venice. Burke noted that "Patronage was most necessary when it was least likely, when a writer was poor, young and unknown" (1986, 114). If a writer found a patron—and most writers used their pens to seek patronage—he might well have entered into the first form that Burke detailed, "the household system [in which] a rich man takes the artist or writer into his house for some years, gives him board, lodging, and presents, and expects to have his artistic and literary needs attended to" (1986, 88). Straparola had tried at least once to secure patronage, from Giacomo Secco in Caravaggio in 1508 or perhaps even before that. If he tried to flatter more exalted rulers not with a short sonnet, but with a lengthy family epic, such as Francesco Filelfo's *Sforziad*, no record survives. During Straparola's lifetime Alvise Cornero of Padua embodied the principal example of literary patronage by collecting and publishing the plays that he had encouraged "Il Ruzzante" to write (Burke 1986, 116).[19]

Patronage could also mean extortion, as in the case of Pietro Aretino, who repeatedly garnered rich gifts from rulers anxious to divert his vitriol from the images they had carefully cultivated for public consumption. But few writers had either Aretino's brazen talent or his remarkable success.

Yet another form of potential patronage consisted of unpublicized rewards for editing nobles' awkward efforts to versify. Letters written in 1539 between one of Straparola's frametale characters, Bernardo Capello, and the marquis del Vasto show the marquis sending a sonnet to Capello for improvement, for which one assumes some form of reward would have been forthcoming (Moro, letters 137, 138, 139, here 138).

Straparola lived in a transitional period as far as literary patronage was concerned. During his lifetime publishers and "the anonymous reading public" were in the process of effectively replacing personal patronage (Burke 1986, 118).[20] Nonetheless, there is every reason to believe that Straparola exchanged his talent for soldi, lira, and perhaps even ducats in a different arena. Consider the experience of the literarily talented Benedetto Varchi (1503–65). He had sent sonnets and epigrams to Ruberto Strozzi (d. 1566), for which Strozzi thanked him because they gave him "a great deal of pleasure." Varchi, with ambitions for his verse, hoped that Strozzi could arrange to have Adriano Willaert set one of his epigrams to music, but Strozzi couldn't promise it. Then Strozzi returned to Varchi with a request for more madrigals:

As I told you, I received the madrigals that you sent me, and they were very pleasing. But having been asked to have another one made in praise of Madonna Pulisena, and having no one else to turn to, I must come to you, and certainly I do it with that boldness with which I would ask one of the women I love [to let me screw her (*chiavarla*): crossed out in ms.] to make love. And therefore I ask you, since you served me so well the first time, not to fail me the second. (Ruberto Strozzi to Benedetto Varchi, 1534, in Chambers and Pullan 1992, 383)

Varchi had written the madrigal and Strozzi had presented it. Whether Strozzi claimed it as his own, we don't know. Now he needed another one. He wanted it in a quite particular form, and he wanted it fast:

Make it in praise of the said Pulisena (who sings very well both in improvising and in reading music), put her name in it, make the two final verses rhyme, and make them eleven syllables apiece, and she would like her name to be mentioned somewhere after the middle of the madrigal. I decided to mention each detail, so that you would not complain as you did last time that I had not explained it to you. So now you can see very well what the lady wants. I leave it to you, who would know better what to do than I what to say.

As the letter proceeded, it emerged that secrecy was paramount, which suggests that Strozzi hoped to offer Varchi's madrigal as his own composition.

I don't want to tell you not to speak to a soul on earth about this, because I would insult you, which certainly would not be right, because I have more faith in you than the Hungarians have in their swords. Let me have it, the sooner the better.

There is no mention of money, but Strozzi was now in Varchi's debt, and in one form or another Varchi undoubtedly eventually collected what he was owed.

It is precisely because there was a ready market for verse of the sort Straparola knew how to produce that the silence of the next thirty-five years is so significant. He would not have stopped writing, but he could easily have stopped writing under his own name, as Benedetto Varchi did here, producing verse, song, enigma, and story for recompense of one sort or another. Varchi was one step removed from the courtesan

Pulisena. Straparola may have occupied much the same position, hearing about beauties-for-pay from others.

Straparola, Venice, and the Mainland from 1508 to 1550

Fixing a geographical location for Straparola's working life for the years between 1515 and 1551 has a linguistic component. It is axiomatic in the study of anthropology that innovation and change move outward from cultural centers and that areas peripheral to cultural centers adopt new habits only later, which can mean months, years, or even generations, depending on the amount and rate of traffic between the cultural center and the outlying areas. Changes in cultural style and language use proceed at different speeds depending on social class, which is a shorthand way of expressing the obvious. Families and individuals with disposable income can afford to associate with trendsetters, to buy newly fashionable clothes, and to learn to speak whatever idiom has been newly introduced.

Giancarlo Mazzacurati points out that Straparola's usage in the *Pleasant Nights* was typical of Venetian literary patterns in the early 1500s and was therefore anachronistic, out-of-date, and old-fashioned when it appeared in 1551 and 1553. Mazzacurati's view supports the hypothesis that Straparola moved among Venetian *literati* at some point after he arrived in Venice. It is reasonable to assume that the first printing of his verse sold sufficiently to warrant a reprinting in 1515, which then led to Straparola's finding, or being offered, a position that took him away from Venice. Straparola's absence from Venice between 1515 and 1549, when he must have begun to compose the *Pleasant Nights*, would account for his out-of-date language and would also be consistent with Mazzacurati's assessment of his literary style.

The discussion up to this point assumes that the language that Straparola produced was *his own* current language rather than a consciously crafted linguistic artifact. I discuss Straparola's prose in greater detail in Chapter 4; it is enough to state here that it is out of the question that the old-fashioned style and language of the *Pleasant Nights* resulted from his, or an editor's, careful editing, given the first-draft, uncorrected, unedited style evident throughout his tales.

Proposing a geographical location for Straparola on the periphery of Venetian power rather than at the very center—that is, in Venice itself—also has a narrative dimension. The most detailed of Straparola's stories treat merchant households. The hypothesis that Straparola was far more familiar with merchant than with noble life in the years between 1515 and 1549 is confirmed by the observation that he seems unfamiliar with the habits and trappings of real power as it would have been exercised at the center of government.

On the mainland, two kinds of households existed where a verbally skilled retainer might find employment, noble and merchant. (It is reasonable to dismiss the households of rich farmers, whose numbers were few and were diminishing in the years between 1515 and 1549.) A noble household might consist of a Venetian family's noninheriting son, his mistress, and their illegitimate children. Because of the usually close ties that bound noble sons to their natal families in Venice, and those sons' probable use of contemporary idiom, the likelihood of Straparola's association with this kind of household is small.

Another possible locus would be a family of the provincial landholding nobility whose primary seat was located on the mainland, not in Venice. There is little to support this possibility either, for none of Straparola's stories betray a landholding vantage point.

A third and far more likely association for Straparola between 1515 and 1549 would have been the household of a wealthy merchant who had commercial ties to Venice. Current studies of living habits and governing patterns in Renaissance Venice and in the Veneto lead me to the conclusion that Straparola spent the decades between the 1515 publication of his *New Works* and the 1549 composition of his *Pleasant Nights* as a literary retainer in a merchant household somewhere in the Veneto, that is, outside Venice itself. The *Pleasant Nights* frametale provides a model for just such a person, the funloving Signor Ferier Beltramo.

Two cities, Padua and Treviso, stand out as likely places to conjecture Straparola's working life. Both were provincial centers of culture with close ties to Venice itself. Like nearly all towns of any size, both Padua and Treviso had literary academies. Paduan men pursued literary pleasure in their literary academies, which because of the University of Padua, included institutions such as the Accademia degli Infiammati for professors and members of Venetian aristocratic intelligentsia (Logan 1972, 73). Trevisan men did the same in the Solleciti and the Perseveranti.[21] In general, however, the intellectual luster of earlier academies had dimmed as sixteenth-century ones became places for members to admire one another's verbal play.

Both cities' municipal lives had undergone radical change, for as the military forces of the League of Cambrai threatened Venice, Treviso's communal government, overseen by Venetian governors, built city walls, diverted the river into the newly constructed moat, and leveled the buildings of the surrounding countryside to deny besiegers refuge. In the ensuing years, commercial life within the city changed fundamentally as it became a city of leisured consumers. Civil disorder and reordering nearly always create unexpected social opportunities, and this was precisely the period in which Straparola would have been seeking a patron.

Investment ties between the mainland and Venice offer another point of entry for considering a possible location for Straparola in these years. Both Padua and Treviso attracted substantial investment in business, housing, and land from families in every one of Venice's six districts, but Padua attracted more investment from Venetian merchants (Gullino 1994).

The overwhelmingly persuasive reason to consider Padua as Straparola's home during the long undocumented period between 1515 and 1549, however, is literary. Paduan is the only dialect other than Bergamesque that appears in the *Pleasant Nights*, where it is the language of the Trevisan's story of Cecato Rabboso and his beautiful wife Tia (night 5, story 4). It is theoretically possible that Straparola could have picked up Paduan from a friend, but living in or near Padua provides by far the more likely source of his knowledge.

In personal terms, the inclusion of the dialect of Straparola's adult life would have provided a neat personal symmetry at the close of Book 1. We may understand the fifth night's stories as including one tale with biographical details that was told in the Bergamesque dialect of his youth, while a second tale was told in the language in which he had functioned on a daily basis up to the moment of composing *Pleasant Nights*. A Paduan life for Straparola is given additional weight by evidence internal to the *Pleasant Nights*, for he, or someone else (see Chapter 4), closed the thirteenth and final story of Book 2 with a Morlini *novella* (# 51) relocated to Padua (Guglielminetti 1979 71). Moreover, Padua was distinguished from other cities mentioned in the *Pleasant Nights* by the cosily familiar terms with which it was described: the Church of St. Anthony was named as Paduans named it, the "chiesa del Santo" (night 13, story 7); the next story (night 13, story 8) took place in the village of Noventa, now called Noventa Padovana, a few kilometers due east of the city; and finally, passage from Padua to Venice occurred, without explanation, simply "per Brenta" (on the River Brenta, night 13, story 13). Surely it is significant that four of the thirteenth night's thirteen stories unfolded in or near Padua. And it *may* be significant that one of Straparola's frametale narrators, Casale, who was indeed Henry VIII's representative, was given a story that took place in two locations, England and Padua!

Within the *Pleasant Nights* Straparola encoded, or had someone else encode, personal as well as peripheral relationships. His printer, Comin da Trino, may have noticed, and have been amused by, the fact that the hero of a story from popular tradition (Rua 1890b, 16,274) became Bertuccio *da Trino* (night 11, story 2). The same is true of Monferrato (the last component in the name of Comin da Trino di Monferrato), a town Straparola had built into two earlier stories.

If Straparola lived in a merchant household in Padua, then he would have had to earn his keep in one way or another. Perhaps the mathematical skills he had learned in his Caravaggio schooldays and the literary skills he had honed in Venice would have been of greater value than any Latin at his disposal. Perhaps he felt close to the ideal represented by Maestro Gotfreddo (night 13, story 12), one of those men whom he characterized as having the judgment to avoid the noxious and to seek out what might be beneficial and profitable. But, the author observed, men like this who were willing to observe certain rules in their manner of life had always been hard to find, and there were few such men left. One senses that Straparola believed that he, or perhaps his merchant patron, was one of those few. And if, like Maestro Gotfreddo, he had risen from rags to comfort by virtue of hard study and high intelligence, and if his efforts had been rewarded with respect based on his virtue and his worth, then we may accept Paul Larivaille's conclusion that Straparola himself strongly identified with the bourgeois careerism for which "Puss in Boots" ("Costantino and His Cat," night 11, story 1) was both an allegory and "un pur hymne à l'arrivisme" (61–62).

Certain it is that Straparola's authorial voice ridiculed unwarranted presumption to learning as it appeared in his rendering of Morlini's tale of Cesare Mota (the tenth story on the thirteenth and final night). Cesare was that most grating of companions, one who thrust his ignorance and memorized facts before the learning of people who had "studied long and diligently." Preposterous, Straparola harrumphed. Worse, however, were wheedlers and flatterers who crowded around anyone with money to spend (night 13, story 13). How painful that might have been to one who valued truth and truth-telling, something Straparola had expressed through the mouth of young Zambò when he replied that he knew only how to till soil and to dress vines. These are observations made with recognizable emotional force. They are also observations that Straparola would have been able to make from a position within a patron's household.

A discussion of emotions that Straparola might have felt leads to a consideration of the person who felt those emotions. Paul Larivaille in his reading of *Pleasant Nights* perceived a set of emotions that to him designated a group without a clearly defined social status, such as subaltern intellectuals, assistants, or teachers (64), a characterization shared by Mario Petrini (1983, 154). Larivaille concludes that these attributes described Straparola's readers; in my view his characterization applies equally well to Straparola himself. Larivaille, who located people with these characteristics in the shadow of the powerful (64), intuitively grasped the nature of emotional relationships as they were implicitly expressed in the *Pleasant Nights*. For Larivaille, such people were not realizing their own potential but lending their powers to their patrons, characterizations that dovetail with the position in which I believe Straparola situated himself or was situated.

I've placed Straparola on the mainland and will leave him there until 1549. Somewhere evidence lurks to confirm or to disprove my hypothesis. Perhaps a study of Padua's literary academies will uncover writing that resembles or is identical to passages Straparola included in his *Opera Nova* or in his *Pleasant Nights*. The search is just beginning.

Who might Straparola's patron have been? He might have been one of the names on a list of Venetians from the Castello, Dorsoduro, San Marco, or Cannaregio districts[22] who owned houses, businesses, land, or leases on land on the mainland in or near Padua. In 1537 they had names like Ambrogio Agugie, Alvise Alemanti, Pasquale dalla Seda, Margherita de Gratia, Marco Frizzier, Costantino Marcora, Pietro Martini, and Bernardino Testa (Gullino 1994 892). Perhaps one or another of them was part of the life of Zoan Francesco Straparola.

Straparola at Mid-Century

Straparola's life must have changed abruptly in 1548 or early 1549. By then he was in his early to mid-sixties, a venerable age in the Renaissance. In all likelihood his patron sickened and died in that year. A patron's death meant "hopes blown away by a puff of wind," as Giorgio Vasari put it in 1537 when his patron died (Burke 1986, 94). If his patron had fathered a son, that child would probably have had little desire to retain a father's gabby old retainer. And if his patron had *not* fathered a child, then Straparola was without hope of continuing employment.

Zoan Francesco Straparola returned to the city of his early hopes, bearing with him the little capital he had managed to accumulate in his years away from Venice.[23] He began writing probably sometime in 1549 (see Chapter 4 for more on the chronology of composition) and received a privilege to protect his work in March 1550. It was in a sense the perfect moment to do so. The early 1550s were the high point in the publishing of literature in Venice (Quondam 1977, 89), just before the Inquisition's censorship clamped down on the press in its efforts to craft morality.

When Straparola first returned to Venice, he may well have witnessed the kind of poverty that Anton Francesco Doni drolly described in a letter to a friend, Girolamo Fava:

We have one bed between the lot of us, and each has his own (O beautiful secret!) chamberpot, because the privies are common to all. . . . To express in a word my state of ease, at one and the same time I can be writing, at table, in bed, or sitting in front of the fire, not to mention in the shithouse. Then I am in every country [at once] and see all mankind if I stand at the window; it looks out onto a place where I can behold Slavs, Greeks, Turks, Moors, Spaniards, Frenchmen, Germans and Italians: different faces, a variety of clothing and weird ways of behaving. . . . I came to Venice in those days to practise printing, . . . I have the most wretched room (if you can call it that) in the whole town, and the worst company, and I suffer the worst discomfort in the world. . . . At night in the manner of a cruel doctor, an army of huge bedbugs, as large as Mocenigos [large silver coins], and a mob of fat fleas, test my pulse and bleed me; above my head, in an old loft, I think there is a college of mice and a consistory of cobwebs; below, there is a street where all night long wretches who waste the daytime pass up and down singing strambotti noisily and certain erotic little madrigals; not to mention [the man next door]. Afflicted by a canker, he energetically struggles, hour after hour, with pills, plasters, embrocations, cupping-glasses, sticky plasters, cauteries, adhesives, wads, and enemas; he shouts at the top of his voice and shits with great difficulty. . . . On the other side of me I have an old woman and a tailor who, what with the noise of the scissors and the coughing of the toothless crone, pass away two thirds of the night for me with pleasures of the most wretched sort to be found in all the world. No sooner is it daybreak than the boats, barges and gondolas appear in a stinking fetid, vile canal, with people shouting and braying with coarse and disjointed voices, competing with each other, one with Brenta water, another with onions and fresh garlic and mouldy melons, rotten grapes, stale fish and green kindling wood, enough to drive crazy everyone of sound mind. (Doni, in Chambers and Pullan 1992, 181–82)

Doni's letter was dated March 1550, the same month in which Straparola received a ten-year protection for his *Pleasant Nights*. If his book didn't succeed, Doni's comically portrayed life might become his own miserably experienced fate.

Since Straparola's book would have to make its way first among Venetian bookbuyers, he praised the city fulsomely. Here are his words from night 5, story 1:

The noble city of Venice, famed for the integrity of its magistrates, for the justice of its laws, and as being the resort of men from every nation in the world ... is named the queen of cities, the refuge of the unhappy, the asylum of the oppressed.

Straparola composed new stories that provided dirt poor girls and boys with a rich future if they enlisted magic to get them well married. When he introduced the fresh young Meldina to his readers, she spoke in his language. She had learned three things in her life, she said. "Do not search for what cannot be found; believe what bears the marks of sense and reason; once you've gotten a rare and precious possession, prize it and keep it close." What profound sadness and regret those words express, if we think of them as Straparola's in old age rather than as Meldina's of tender years. Doing well now was a matter of selling a book. Straparola cast his net broadly and wrote for an entire city. He retold tales that had long been in print; he, or someone he knew, translated many from Latin, and he created visions of hope—his rise tales— for the poor.

After Zoan Straparola had finished the manuscript and had received his privilege, he went to Comin da Trino, one of Venice's largest printers and at mid-century probably the most active in Venice (Grendler 1977, 17; Donvito 1997, 1: 310), and he began the negotiations that resulted in the publication of *Pleasant Nights*. The book's first date of publication is usually listed as "1550" because that date appears in the colophon and "2 January 1550" dates the address to readers. But because the year began on March 1, "2 January 1550" by our calendar would be 2 January 1551.

Straparola placed the books with a bookseller at the sign of Santa Alvise, where they sold so briskly that the first print run was quickly depleted. Comin da Trino had his workers reset the type[24] for a second printing of Book 1 later in the same year, 1551, probably in a print run of 1000 copies (Grendler 1977, 9). He placed it with a bookseller we can precisely locate, for the shop was at San Luca at the sign of the Diamante. It was in the bookselling district in the center of the city, which was "bounded by the districts of San Marco, Sant'Angelo, Rialto Bridge, Santi Apostoli, San Zanipolo (=Giovanni e Paolo) and Santa Maria Formosa" (Grendler 1977, 5).

In 1553 Zoan finished work on volume 2, dating his foreword 1 September. In it he lashed out at unnamed attackers of his work, who—whether motivated by jealousy or by sheer malice—had claimed he'd stolen the stories that he had written (*da me scritte*). He "confessed" he'd faithfully written them according to the way in which they'd been told by ten "damigelle" (young women, A ii[r]). And then he continued in an age-old self-effacing trope: he'd not produced these stories out of overweening pride or from the wish to acquire honor and reputation, but solely to amuse the gracious and lovely ladies (amorevoli donne) to whom he had addressed these words. He ended with a greeting: "Be happy, remember those on whose hearts you are engraved, not the least of whom I believe myself to be."[25]

Two sold-out printings of Book 1 may have netted Straparola a tidy sum. He had lived his life in other people's shadow, but now he could claim a space for himself and could memorialize himself. And so Zoan, now a more dignified Giovan Francesco, departed from the functionality of popular print (Barberi 1969, 1: 82) and had a portrait inserted on the page facing his introduction (Figure 3). No name identifies it. No name needs to identify it, for only Straparola can be meant by it. Stylized, all-purpose busts could be had to lend dignity to a book's appearance,[26] but those authorial "portraits" were generally set in elaborately architectonic or mythological baroque frames, like the one surrounding a portrait of Girolamo Ruscelli that Comin da Trino printed some years later (Mortimer 1996, 50).[27] Like the authorial portrait of Niccolò Martelli that Antonio Francesco Doni put on the front of his volume of Martelli's letters (Mortimer 1996, 49), or Doni's own repeatedly produced portrait (Doni 1572, 1575), the Straparola portrait exemplified mid-sixteenth-century realism. Hair cropped, beard long, the head and shoulders portrait has scowling eyes narrowed in disapproval,

Figure 3. Frontispiece, woodcut portrait of Straparola from *Piacevoli Notti*, Book 2 (Venice: Comin da Trino, 1556). Reproduced by permission of Nationalbibliothek, Vienna.

perhaps distrust. In an age in which authorial portraits became increasingly true to life (Barberi 1969, cited in Richardson 1999, 101), it pictured a man who was not at ease with the world.

One year, four months, and eleven days later, on 11 January 1555,[28] Straparola signed his last dated foreword. Directed toward the same "amorevole (sic) donne" whom he had previously addressed, the same words now seem tired and sad. Once again he defended his authorship and tooted his own horn about the enigmas (*gli enimmi dell ingenioso mess Gioanfrancesco (sic) Straparola da Caravaggio nomen elegante*). At this point in his life he knew he was no Petrarch and he acknowledged his low style (*il basso & rimesso stile dello autore*, A iii^r). In the familiar old trope he reminded readers that he had reproduced these stories against the will of the storytellers. That this too is part of a standard disclaimer is borne out by the fact that most of the named worthies were dead by 1551 and could hardly have objected. The foreword's final words were those of a sick old man who knew that death was nearing. He had used them in 1551, but now they seemed especially poignant: "Be happy and remember me."[29]

In the winter of 1555–56 plague ravaged Venice. In fleeing the plague, he may well have returned to the mainland town in which he had lived for so many years. He directed Comin da Trino to print another edition, as the printer indicated when for the last time he included the words, "All'instanza dall'autore" (at the behest of the author) in the printing of 1555, "1556," and "1557."

After that Straparola's voice fell silent and his portrait disappeared. He did not die in Venice, for his name does not appear there on any necrology in the 1550s or the early 1560s.[30] If necrologies still exist from the 1550s in mainland municipalities, it is there that the end of his life lies recorded.

4

Straparola at His Desk

BOOK I AND BOOK 2 OF THE *Pleasant Nights* differ so profoundly from one another that it is impossible to hold that the stories of both books were composed in a single creative effort. In the Rua edition he stories of Book 1 average 10 pages in length, those of Book 2 average 6 pages in length for nights 6–10 and diminish dramatically to an average of 3 pages per story in the final three nights[1] (see Table 1).

The fact that Book 1 contains five nights strongly suggests that Straparola originally intended a ten-night sequence of stories like that produced by his illustrious predecessor Giovanni Boccaccio. The reduced lengths of stories in nights 6 through 10 indicate that Straparola's creative energy faltered in Book 2. To fill out the manuscript and bring it up to the length of Book 1, he composed his masterpiece "Costantino and His Cat" as the first story of the eleventh night. Then he gave up. From this point onward the stories—with one exception—tumbled

TABLE I. Average page lengths by night, Books 1, 2 (Rua edition).

Book 1					Book 2							
1	2	3	4	5	6	7	8	9	10	11	12	13
		X										
X		X	X	X								
X	X	X	X	X								
X	X	X	X	X								
X	X	X	X	X				X				
X	X	X	X	X	X	X	X	X	X			
X	X	X	X	X	X	X	X	X	X			
X	X	X	X	X	X	X	X	X	X	X		
X	X	X	X	X	X	X	X	X	X	X	X	
X	X	X	X	X	X	X	X	X	X	X	X	X
X	X	X	X	X	X	X	X	X	X	X	X	X

LE PIACEVOLI

NOTTI DI M. GIOVAN-
francesco Straparola da
Carauaggio

298

NELLE QVALI SI CONTEN-
gono le fauole con i loro enimmi da
dieci donne, & duo giouani raccontate, cofa diletteuole,
ne piu data in luce.

CON PRIVILEGIO.

LVX FVLGET IN TENEBRI

APPRESSO ORPHEO DALLA
carta tien per infegna.S.Aluife.
M. D. L.

t. I.

Figure 4. Title page of first edition of *Piacevoli Notti*. Reproduced by permission of Beinecke Rare Book and Manuscript Library, Yale University.

at random off the pages of a 1520 edition of Morlini's *Novellae* into
Straparola's book, even maintaining Morlini's punctuation as the translation progressed (Villani 1982, 69) but in other respects simplifying,
secularizing, and occasionally relocating the stories (Guglielminetti
1979, 76, 78).

The differences between Books 1 and 2 bespeak discontinuous
composition and support the hypothesis that the manuscript Straparola
submitted to the commission that granted him a ten-year privilege was
not complete, but only Book 1's stories, surrounding frametale, songs,
and enigmas. There are narrative and content breaks within Book 2
and jarring factual errors in the frametale, which together suggest that
Straparola's collection was completed with significant participation
from someone else, while the fact that he continued to have the book
printed and published at his own behest (*ad instanza dall'autore*) is
convincing evidence that he returned to physical competence after the
manuscript had been completed.

Sources and Readership Appeal

Scholars recognize that the *Pleasant Nights* has a highly complex textual
and editorial genealogy (Leclerc 1993, 31; Jannet in Straparola 1857,
Introduction).[2] In nights 1 through 10 Straparola picked and chose
among a variety of sources for his stories, most of which were ably identified in 1890 by Giuseppe Rua in a lengthy article in the *Giornale Storico
dello Letteratura Italiana* (Rua 1890b, 16: 218–83). These stories demonstrate that Straparola had a broad and inclusive knowledge of Italy's
narrative tradition.

To understand Straparola's working method, we need to recon-
stitute his thinking in the spring, summer, and autumn of 1549, and
again in 1552, as he considered how to construct and what to put into
his collection of stories. Social, literary, publishing, and art histories
of Renaissance Venice give some idea of the kinds of general literary
knowledge that Straparola would have shared with potential readers;
they also give some idea of what else was for sale in the literary marketplace as Straparola began work on the *Pleasant Nights*.

Fabliaux and medieval stories, characterized by a now unfamiliar
physical directness about sex and scatology, remained popular in Renaissance Venice as they also did in other parts of Europe. Elite readers read

fabliaux in Latin, common readers in Italian. To judge from other tale collections circulating at mid-century, fabliaux were as ubiquitous as animal tales, like the Aesopic fables that had long been part of elementary school curricula in Italy (Griffante 1994, 315–40).

High literature for mid-sixteenth-century readers meant Boccaccio, Petrarch, and Dante. Of these three stars in the literary firmament, it was Boccaccio who was regarded as the father of Italian literature in terms of style and content and whose influence was most evident in the *Pleasant Nights*. Like the majority of tale collection authors before him, Straparola had mined the *Decameron* for material and had mimicked its structure, easy enough to do, as one edition after another of the *Decameron* appeared between 1500 and 1550.

A literature more popular in form and content offered Italians in general and Venetians in particular the adventures of Orlando, Rinaldo, and Angelica in Matteo Maria Boiardo's (ca. 1440–94) *Orlando Inamorato* and Ludovico Ariosto's (1474–1533) *Orlando Furioso*. These romances could also be heard in municipally supported performances in public spaces, because municipalities had for decades hired singers and storytellers to perform courtly romances publicly. To musical accompaniment, entertainers sang from the printed page and afterward hawked copies of the texts they had just performed (Lowry 1992, 34; Corrigan 1976, 6; Richardson 1999, 73), texts with the built-in "orality" of phrases like "I tell the story" and "I'll sing the old and beautiful story" (Lommatzsch 1950, 1: 26, 3: 27; see also the text of *Lionbruno*). Their heroes (like Pirramo, Giasone, Guiscardo, Orlando, and Lionbruno), their heroines (like Tisbe, Medea, Gismonda, Angelica, and Madonna Aquilina), and their adventures were the mainstay of the broad public's literary diet, with a few fairies and giants thrown in for dessert.

It is consistent with the differentness of Straparola's newly composed rise tales that he regularly referred to all of his books' narratives not as *novelle*, as Boccaccio and subsequent tale collection writers had done, but as *favole* (Cottino-Jones 2000, 176), a less esteemed genre. His word choice provides a sure indication that he was conscious of the fact that his narrative composition diverged from traditional narratives.

When widespread schooling brought literacy to younger readers, female readers, less well-educated readers, and eventually readers among the urban proletariat (Richardson 1994, 91; 1999, 109–11), rich bookselling opportunities opened. Boys and men (who accounted for the largest number of Italy's urban readers) and girls and women formed a market for mass-produced books, and they were hungry for new stories.[3] The existence of a socially diverse and gender-mixed reading public probably played a role in Straparola's choice of stories and the design of his books' frametale.

In the mid-1500s, books that had proven themselves in the literary marketplace were ones like *Orlando inamorato* and *Orlando furioso*, which had been published and republished in the 1500s and continued to be popular as Straparola was composing his collection. He would have been justified in concluding that the verse romance market was saturated. If so, he would have been convinced that he would need to produce a new and different literary product to be able to compete successfully in the Venetian literary market.

The stories in *Pleasant Nights* show Straparola casting his imaginative net widely. From the ancient world he borrowed from Ovid's *Metamorphoses* (Clausen-Stolzenburg 1995, 335), available in Italian as *Methamorphoses vulgare hystoriado* since 1508. Story elements from Lucius Apuleius's *Golden Ass* were also well represented in the *Pleasant Nights*, but Straparola wouldn't have needed to use Latin to search out plots to borrow, because Boiardo had already translated Apuleius's classic into Italian, and it had appeared as *L. Apvlegio tradotto in volgare* in 1549. Straparola's own knowledge of the Roman classics extended to the Roman tale of the daughter who nourished her imprisoned father with her own milk, a plot that he built into Lionora's enigma (night 7, story 5); he was sufficiently familiar with Greek mythology to introduce Clotho, Lachesis, and Atropos smoothly into another enigma (night 4, story 5) and to put a satyr into yet another (night 4, story 1). He slipped the Roman Latona into the Proem of the fifth night; he borrowed that quintessential image of Greek tragedy—the tearing of hair, ripping of dresses, and baring of breasts—for the behavior of Doralice's children's nurses (night 1, story 4).[4] Straparola's frequent references to Greek and Roman mythology suggest that his classical education was alive and well. However, we should be cautious and should not all too credulously ascribe a vast knowledge of classics to Straparola, for our Renaissance forbears *wished* to appear learned in the classics (Grafton 1985, 615–49). Whether or not they knew Latin, Straparola—and other Venetians—would have easily picked up Roman and Greek mythology from the depictions of gods, goddesses, and their histories painted in and on public buildings. Since classical mythology formed a prominent part of urban visual culture, Straparola's naming of gods and goddesses—in judicious moderation—fit comfortably into familiar elements of Venetian life and would have probably added to the salability of his collection.

Straparola plundered the late fourteenth-century *Gesta Romanorum* for plots, like many authors before him. More medieval materials lay ready to hand in Boiardo's embroidered and elaborated accounts of Charlemagne's heroic vassal Orlando (Roland). First printed during Straparola's youth as *Orlando inamorato*, Boiardo's verse romance celebrated military valor and religious ideals. Wildly popular, it was performed publicly so frequently that eventually it engendered parodies, such as *La polenta*, in which Orlando died not from being wounded in battle, but from eating too much polenta (Lommatzsch 1950, 1: 171–76)! In the following decades, Boiardo's *Orlando inamorato* was joined by Ariosto's sequel *Orlando furioso*. Published in 1516, the year after Straparola's own *New Works* had appeared for the second time, Ariosto's Orlando narrative captured the public's imagination with its classic fables, tales from the Arthurian cycle, and elements from Charlemagne epics. It was eminently suitable for expansion and addition: Ariosto himself added to it in 1531, and so did other authors in later years. Its repeated printings in the 1530s and 1540s would have alerted Straparola to the fact that Ariosto's versions of Arthurian romance were familiar to readers in Venice as well as to provincial readers on the mainland.

If we ponder Straparola's reasons for wishing to publish a book of stories, two obvious possibilities spring to mind. The first was money, because investing in a successful book had the potential for bringing its author substantial returns. Straparola may well have set aside something for his old age, because the few hints we can garner from the production of his *Pleasant Nights* tell us that it was neither a printer nor a patron who funded its printing. In an age in which authors actively sought patronage, if such a patron had existed, Straparola would have openly named him, publicly praised him, and gratefully thanked him. There was, however, neither name nor praise nor gratitude, and, therefore, there was no patron whose largesse cushioned the aged Straparola from having to make a living in a harsh commercial world.

A second reason for publishing a collection of stories was fame, reputation, and the good opinion of contemporaries. This would have been particularly important for someone, who—as I surmised in Chapter 3—had sold his literary gifts during most of his life. Now he, like eminent men who published their poetry or personal letters, could give voice to his indwelling talents under his own name.

Planning Publication

Like contemporary authors, Straparola would have entered into discussions with a bookseller about a manuscript's marketability. In this case I imagine that Straparola first went to someone he knew in the bookshop "At the Sign of Saint Alvise," which was where most printings of Book 1 sold during Straparola's lifetime, while a bookstore called "The Little Dove" just behind the great Fondaco dei Tedeschi sold Book 2.[5]

STRAPAROLA: I'm composing a new collection of stories, like Boccaccio's but at night. There're going to be ten nights,[6] and I'll call it *Pleasant Nights*. *Pleasant*, you know, *Piacevoli*, like the books that Comin da Trino did, *I Piacevoli Discorsi* and *Il rimanente de le piacevole e ingegnose lettere*.

BOOKSELLER: "Pleasant"—that's good. What else?

STRAPAROLA: It's set here in Venice . . . not *now*, of course . . . might make problems . . . in Murano about ten years ago. What do you think?

BOOKSELLER: Sounds interesting. Who's your market?

STRAPAROLA: Mainly people who've been buying the Orlando stories . . . I think my stories are just as good, better even . . . Ariosto's Orlando stories sell, but really they're just a bit of this and a bit of that, galloping around forests . . .

BOOKSELLER: Maybe. But those stories sell.[7] Orlando's not the only one—look at *L'Antheo, Selvette, Ciriffo, Guerrin*[8] . . . If you're going to have—how many stories did you say. . . ?

STRAPAROLA: . . . I'm planning 50 altogether . . .

BOOKSELLER: Are any of them romances?

STRAPAROLA: There *are* a few romance-type stories, but I've written some new stories, where poor people get rich.

BOOKSELLER: How? Nobody's getting rich these days.

STRAPAROLA: I don't mean getting rich in the usual way. I mean getting rich by magic. My stories are about poor people—some boys, some girls, men, women—and they end up marrying princesses and kings, of course, nobody like the Vendramins or the Loredans.

BOOKSELLER: What can I say . . . this is an untested market . . . you don't have a name here in Venice, either . . . that's another risk. But I'll carry it for you if you bring me the printed sheets. Who's going to print the book?

STRAPAROLA: I thought I'd go to Comin da Trino.

BOOKSELLER: He's good. Let me know how it works out. By the way, have you got a dedication or a recommendation? Who's going to write it for you?

STRAPAROLA: Nobody . . . yet. . . .

BOOKSELLER: Never mind. Comin can do that, or one of his editors.

With a bookseller assured, even if Straparola had to shoulder all the expenses, he would have been ready to take the next step. The following conversation that I've imagined between Straparola and Comin da Trino is based on standard Renaissance Venetian printing practice (Grendler 1977; Richardson 1994, 1999), which at mid-century still regarded oral agreements as binding contracts.

Comin da Trino, like so many of Venice's bookmen, was an immigrant from the provinces, in his case, from Monferrato, a small town near Brescia. He'd been in business in Venice near St. John Chrysostom in the Cannaregio district of Venice (Donvito 1997, 311) a little more than ten years when he printed Straparola's Book 1. His small octavo and quarto books were distinguished by elegant typography framed by generous margins (Donvito 1997, 314). In business terms, he typically took printing orders from booksellers; sometimes, however, he copublished with booksellers or, very rarely, took complete technical and commercial responsibility for printing a book (Richardson 1999, 34–35).

In approaching Comin da Trino, Straparola was going to a printer with a large list of vernacular works. He had reprinted Pietro Bembo's influential 1505 *Asolani* in 1540, as well as verse by Antonio Molino. Might it be relevant, or even significant, that both Bembo and Molino appear in Straparola's frame tale?

In discussion with Straparola, Comin da Trino would have probably incorporated characteristically Venetian turns of phrase, while still speaking with the provincial accent of his home town. A businessman at the height of his business success who found himself in conversation with a literary unknown, he would have responded bluntly and directly to Straparola's description of his project:

COMIN DA TRINO: It sounds as though the book you're proposing is going to take about 40 to 50 sheets for the ten nights. If we do a thousand copies, and that's pretty standard, that's 80 to 100 reams, and that'll be 70, maybe 75 ducats.[9] You might need some financing, at least for the paper. Then we'll need a printer with an apprentice for 40 days' work and there's the ink.

STRAPAROLA: That's a lot of money.

COMIN DA TRINO: There's another possibility—how about printing the first five nights and seeing how it sells? In any case, you're going to need a bookseller. Have you got a bookseller yet? You know I work with Zenaro at the Fountain and Arrivabene at the Well. There's also Paolo Gherardo at the Eagle, Michelangelo Biondo, and those guys at the Clock and at the Palm.[10]

STRAPAROLA: I talked with Bonfadini at the Diamond—he'll carry it. [See below.]

COMIN DA TRINO: I'd rather deal with the people at Saint Alvise or at the Little Dove. Do you know them? By the way, there's no religion in this, is there?

They called me in a few months ago about a catechism I did, and I don't
want any more of *that*.[11]

STRAPAROLA: Don't worry. There's not going to be any religion in this book.

After a similar conversation, Straparola probably made inquiries at a
number of booksellers about placing printed sheets for sale on their
premises, and ended up making a binding agreement with the bookseller at the sign of Saint Alvise for Book 1.

The Stories

Straparola's stories are now an accomplished fact, but in 1549/50 the
collection was at most a glimmer in an old man's eye. He began thematically, in a rough sort of way: the first five stories for the first night's
storytelling were mostly about rewards, something that must have been
a pressing hope as Straparola began his work. With one eye on the
robust and boisterous public he hoped would buy his books, his stories
rewarded knavery and cunning as well as virtue.

On the second night Straparola launched his first newly composed
rise tale, "Prince Pig." He wanted to show how a poor girl could rise
from poverty to the wealth of royalty, but the plot was only a rough
beginning for what would eventually become the most popular kind
of Western fairy tale. Straparola told his tales according to values he
understood. "Prince Pig," like other tales in the *Pleasant Nights*, rested
on the assumption that people could be casually disposed of. Central
to this tale, this view emerged more than once in the *Pleasant Nights*.
Prince Pig killed the first and second of three sisters on their wedding
nights, acts that Straparola justified on the grounds that each one
had herself intended to kill her pigskinned husband. The third sister
Meldina, however, accepted her beastly groom—mud, slime, pigskin,
and all—and was rewarded with motherhood and eventual queenship.[12]

One after the other, the second night's stories similarly dealt with
problematic relationships between men and women. A man mortified
three women who had rejected him sexually by exposing their naked
bodies to their husbands' voyeurism (night 2, story 2); a woman defended her virginity against a rapacious monarch (night 2, story 3); the
nagging of Silvia Balestro drove the devil back to hell in a story with
which Straparola thought his readers might not be familiar (night 2,
story 4); and a husband came to value his wife in the process of driving

off an admirer (night 2, story 5). As suitable as these stories were for readers in Renaissance Venice, they would grate painfully on the tenderer sensibilities of eighteenth-century censors, which caused them to fall from fashion.

For the third night of storytelling Straparola again began with a story of his own creation, "Pietro Pazzo." This time he chose a poor *boy*—not good-looking and virtuous like Meldina, but ugly, rude, and stupid. It was a description with the potential to cultivate a reassuring sense of superiority among its readers, in whom the story was well suited to fostering a gratifying sense of being better looking, better bred, and more intelligent than the titular hero Pietro the Fool. If a repellently filthy and stupid boy could marry a princess with the help of a little magic, readers might feel encouraged to imagine or dream of an even more glorious future for themselves. The next three stories Straparola chose for the third night were also magic tales, but of the long familiar restoration variety (see Chapter 1). The last was a lusty folktale in which avarice brought down a wicked and dissolute woman.

On the fourth night Straparola alternated restoration magic tales with urban tales of love and cuckoldry, closing the session with an exemplum about reaching out to life and fleeing death.

For the fifth night Straparola turned away from urban tales of rascality and opted once again for magic. The first, a restoration tale, showed Guerrino regaining his royal status by magic means. The second, another of Straparola's own tales, detailed Adamantina's rise from penury to prosperity with the help of a magic doll. The first half of the third one reflected Straparola's own life and concluded with a widely known plot about a body that refused (or appeared to refuse) to be disposed of. The last two stories were about women and their lovers, the first a tale of cunning ribaldry (night 5, story 4), the second an arch morality tale (night 5, story 5).

The Frametale

When Straparola began his collection, it was obvious that he would have to invent a frametale situation. Italy's—and Europe's—long-accepted frametale convention required a group of people who were isolated from surrounding society for a limited period of time. Boccaccio, the most famous storyteller in Italy, had moved ten storytellers from Florence to a country villa to escape the plague. Chaucer had sent a cross-section of English society on a pilgrimage from Southwark to Canterbury. Straparola needed a socially plausible group of people whose names his readers would recognize but who had lived far enough in the past—or who were now dead—so that he could refer to them freely without fear of social repercussion. Moreover, their venue shouldn't be in the center of Venice, where every urban palace was well known, but sufficiently distant so that the location could be known in general terms, but not in specific detail.

Since Straparola had chosen nights rather than days for storytelling, he provided evening pursuits for the storytellers and their company. The group would assemble, dance, sing, choose storytellers by lot, tell stories, propound and try to solve enigmas, dine on sweetmeats and rare wines. Then the evening would end, everyone dispersing by the light of torches (Proem to first night; night 1, story 5).

In choosing Murano, Straparola repeated the choice of Giovanni Sercambi (1347–1424), who had used the same island for his band of storytellers in his *Novellae*. By 1549 Murano had even more palaces where a storytelling troupe might gather. The oppressive heat of the Venetian summer could return in the autumn, and perhaps it did so as Straparola began to work on the collection in the autumn of 1549. At any rate, it crept unnoticed and uncorrected into his anachronistic description of impossible late winter "din and heat" during the city's Venetian Carneval season (Proem).

Straparola needed a historical occasion for the gathering of his storytellers, and this he chose with great care. Unlike Boccaccio and Chaucer who had created storytelling events that took place in their own day, Straparola chose an event from the past, albeit from the relatively recent past. Then he populated that event with people most of whom had died in the meantime. Chief among them was Ottaviano Maria Sforza (1477–1541?), son of Galeazzo Sforza, duke of Milan (1449–1476). Galeazzo had been murdered in 1476,[13] and his first legitimate son Gian Galeazzo (1469–94) succeeded to the dukedom as a child of seven. However, his uncle Ludovico the Moor (1451–1508) soon usurped power. When Ludovico died in 1508, the legitimate heir, Gian Galeazzo, had been dead for fourteen years and his only legitimate brother, Ermes, had been dead for five years. Gian Galeazzo had a legitimate son who survived him, but by then the duchy was effectively controlled by outside forces, either by the French or by the Hapsburgs. They were, as Straparola wrote in the Proem, evil times.

Ottaviano Maria Sforza (1477–1541?), Duke Galeazzo's last, and illegitimate, child, was born after his father's death, and as an illegitimate son was in no way the heir to the duchy of Milan. Despite that fact, Straparola consistently described him as "the Duke." The real Ottaviano Maria was given a bishopric in 1497 in Lodi, a small town 30 kilometers southeast of Milan, on the political boundary between the territories of Milan and Venice, and only about 25 kilometers from Caravaggio itself. The people of Lodi, however, were unhappy at the appointment, and Ottaviano Maria returned to private life in 1533. The bishopric reverted to the Holy Roman Empire in 1535, and Ottaviano Maria left Lodi in a hurry.

Straparola told the story differently. Loyally calling Ottaviano Maria "the Duke," he cited malevolent Milanese relatives as the force that drove him from Lodi. Straparola also got other parts of the history of the duchy of Milan wrong. Francesco Sforza was not the immediate "predecessor" of Ottaviano Maria, nor was Lucrezia a legitimate daughter of Ottaviano Maria, although that did not prevent her —in actual fact—from marrying a minor Gonzaga.[14] In Straparola's version of his history, however, when Ottaviano Maria Sforza fled to Venice he and his daughter accepted the hospitality of a Trevisan merchant, Ferier Beltramo (died 1537; Pirovano in Straparola 2000, 1: 6n3).

A convenient ambiguity surrounded the identity of Ottaviano Maria's daughter, Lucrezia, in Straparola's frametale. Another Lucrezia, born a Gonzaga, had married a cousin of the famous Federico II, son to Isabella d'Este. In her youth *this* Lucrezia Gonzaga (not Lucrezia the daughter of Ottaviano Maria Sforza) had been tutored by the great Italian storyteller, Matteo Bandello (1485–1562), whom at the glittering Gonzaga court of Mantua some thirty years before she had commanded to compose and then to recite stories. At the time that Straparola was compiling *his* collection, this Lucrezia Gonzaga was also a widow.

The similarities of name and condition of the two Lucrezias were convenient ones for Straparola. By including a "Lucrezia Gonzaga" who commanded the telling of tales in the frametale he had created, Straparola evoked the brilliant court of Mantua—which highly placed readers would have known or remembered as the home of Lucrezia Gonzaga. This was at best a disingenuous melding of Lucrezias, for Straparola would have known that a woman born as Lucrezia Sforza would have retained that name throughout her life; that is, she would not have become known as "Lucrezia Gonzaga" because she had married a Gonzaga. Nonetheless, the names evoked one another. Lucrezia Gonzaga had been responsible for Bandello's legendary (but not yet published) stories; another Lucrezia [Sforza] Gonzaga moved a later storyteller, Straparola, to do the same. For those in the know, the narrative situation covertly equated Straparola with Bandello. Was this a subtle self-referential allusion that Straparola had calculatingly worked into the frametale? Or was it an opportunistic conflation of two different Lucrezias, easily made because of the complicated history of northern Italy's many ruling houses? Or did Straparola learn of "Lucrezia [Sforza] Gonzaga" in stories told about Giacomo Secco, whom Straparola so admired, who was himself the beloved nephew of Caterina Gonzaga (Secco 1968, 195)? Perhaps as young Zoan grew up on the streets of Caravaggio he had overheard excited reports of "their" Giacomo's exploits among the famous Mantuan Gonzagas.

Northern Italy's ruling families made covert appearances in *Pleasant Nights*, appearances that the humble among Straparola's readers may not have recognized. For example, Straparola memorialized Ottaviano Maria's aunts and uncles by distributing their unusual names—Isotta, Polissena, Drusiana, Galeazzo, Polidoro, Ippolita, Filippo, Fiordelisa, Ascanio, Elisabetta, Bianca Francesca, Bona Francesca (but not Ludovico il Moro) among the characters of his tales.[15] Those names belong to the generation *before* Ottaviano Maria Sforza, a generation more contemporary with Giacomo Secco, who had served the Gonzagas, as had his father Antonio (1420–80) and both uncles, Francesco (1423–96) and Stefano (n.d.). Most of Ottaviano's own brothers and sisters had humdrum names that don't stand out in any sense: Carlo, Caterina, Allessandro, Bianca Maria, Anna Maria. In choosing names for his characters, Straparola also ignored the hometown Caravaggio branch of the Sforza family. Instituted only in 1497, this dynasty came into existence at about the time that Straparola left Caravaggio for Venice. In any case, it was a noble line created by the hated usurper Ludovico for his illegitimate son Giampaolo, and as such the Caravaggio Sforzas weren't likely to have inspired either affection or loyalty in Straparola.

Having manufactured an easily identifiable location and a memorable occasion for "telling" the stories he had picked out and put together, Straparola needed an audience. This he gathered from eminent Venetian men of letters, all of them then famous and some still

well known. There were two bishops, a doctor of arts, a poet, and as
Straparola put it, many nobles and men of learning (Proem). Chief
among them was Gregorio Casale (ca. 1490–1536), a Bolognese church-
man who acted as an envoy between Henry VIII and Venice. In his
capacity as an ambassador he occupied first place among the men who
were present. Next was the brilliant and nobly born Pietro Bembo
(1470–1547), renowned for his celebration of Italian vernacular literature. A monsignor at the time of the reputed Murano gathering, his
offices—as Venice's official historian and librarian of St. Mark's Cathedral—marked him as a man of exceptional literary merit; in 1539 he
was raised to the College of Cardinals, in the robes of which august
position Titian portrayed him white-bearded a few years later. As a
younger man Bembo had appeared, again as the *second* most eminent
speaker, in Baldassar Castiglione's *Courtier*, and it may well have been
his position there that Straparola borrowed for his own book.

Straparola's description of the Murano gathering sounds like memory and longing joined to produce a wistful nostalgia. His "memories" of the merry company sound emotionally true, because his words
suggest an intimate knowledge of gatherings like the happy ones
he described. And yet many of his wistful words come straight from
Boccaccio's *Decameron*, as, for example, when his women and men
laughed so loudly, and it seemed they were still laughing.[16]

Even if Straparola borrowed phrases from Boccaccio, the nights he
described could still have been nights on which his own stories had
been told, just as Bandello's had been at gatherings in Mantua. Straparola's then-patron might have begged him for something new for him
to tell. Perhaps one of the men named in this company was the very
patron in whose shadow Straparola had spent his productive years and
whose recent death had cast him adrift. Infused with a sense of evenings
experienced either directly or through hearsay, the reported words and
actions of Pietro Bembo seem fresh and direct: Bembo complimented
the storyteller on her appearance on the fifth night (story 2); washed his
hands before a dinner of delicate dishes and new wines (night 5, story
5); along with the Signor Ambassador, accompanied Signora Lucrezia
as she led the way into dinner. Another guest, Vangelista de Cittadini,
was a bishop who served Cardinal Triulzi as secretary and whom Bembo
knew in real life (Rua 1890a, 137n1; Pirovano in Straparola 2000, 1:
9n4), as he also knew Bernardo Capello (Guglielminetti 1984, 33).

Several men at the Murano gathering were musically talented.

Benedetto Trivigiano and Antonio Molino (1495–1571) regularly played the lute and sang. An actor, comic author, and minor poet, Trivigiano, nicknamed Burchiella, took great enjoyment in reciting the tales Straparola gave him.[17] Did his listeners think his humor resembled that of the Florentine satirist Burchiello (Domenico di Giovanni, 1404–49)? Did they think he looked like a canal barge (*burchio* or *burchiello*)?

Finally there was the fugitive bishop Ottaviano Maria Sforza. He had occasioned the Murano gathering and should have appeared in the frametale, but he was not there. Once his flight to Murano had set the storytelling sessions going, he disappeared without explanation, quietly and completely.

Did such a gathering in the form rendered here actually take place? The answer to that question is complicated. All of the men Straparola brought together in the frametale were socially linked in real life through their acquaintance with Pietro Bembo or with Pietro Aretino, two men who also knew one another (Rua 1890, 15: 137n1, 138–39). The reality of these men's documentable interrelationships makes it theoretically possible that in real life Straparola actually witnessed gatherings at which they were present. But were *all* the men named in the frametale present at the *same* time at the kind of gathering Straparola described in the *Pleasant Nights*? The answer to that question is an unequivocal "no," because there is no single date at which all the named men were alive, available, and in Venice. Giuseppe Rua suggested 1536 as a possible date, because in that year Ottaviano Maria was in Venice, from which he wrote a letter to cardinal Caracciolo dated 8 August 1536. Casale, on the other hand, died sometime in the second half of 1536, and by 22 April 1537 Ottaviano Maria was no longer in Venice but in Crema, where he was still to be found in early June 1537 (Rua 1890a, 135, 140n1). In addition, as Donato Pirovano has pointed out, Pietro Bembo was in Padua and Casale was in prison in the first half of that year (Pirovano in Straparola 2000, 1:10n2), which destroys the last remaining possibility for such a gathering to have taken place as Straparola described it. Even though Ottaviano Maria returned to Venice in July 1537 and was still on Murano on 1 January 1538 (Rua 1890a, 136), a date often cited for the fictive gathering, Casale was by then long dead.

One of the strongest arguments against regarding the *Pleasant Nights* as a faithful record of a storytelling event with the people named in its frametale lies in the text of Book 1's letter from "Orfeo dalla Carta alla piacevoli, et amorose donne." There the author of the dedicatory letter, whom I understand to have been Comin da Trino or one of his editors, distanced himself from the stories' "low" (*basso*) style.[18] He did so by attributing it to the ladies who had told the stories. This discourteous characterization of the literary abilities and taste of Straparola's "lovely ladies" smacks of a reluctant printer wishing to preserve his reputation for printing prose of high quality, but it undermined the fictive gathering's elegance Straparola himself had labored to create. It's difficult to imagine that Straparola would have allowed the word "basso" to stand had it in fact referred to a real group of people whom he had known as intimately as the frametale intimated.

Scrutiny of the truth factor of Straparola's description of the frametale gathering must also take the fallibility of human memory into account. At most, readers are justified in accepting the brief presence of the Sforza father/daughter duo on Murano, occasionally in the company of the men named, a group possibly conflated in Straparola's memory from individual occasions. On the other hand, the presiding Signora, delighted though she was said to be at the sight of fish darting about in the water beneath her balcony, was not described with a single word. The strange absences of description corroborate another frametale failing on Straparola's part. The entire world of Pietro Bembo's correspondents, one of whom was Veronica Gambara, a respectable woman like the Signora (Moro passim; Perocco 1985 passim), addressed Pietro Bembo as "Monsignor" in the 1520s and 1530s (Perocco 1985 passim). Straparola never did that. It was as if that important fact did not signify for him. That could only mean that, like the Signora, he hadn't encountered Bembo personally but only by hearsay, yet another reason for considering the personnel of the "remembered" frametale not historical fact but considered fabrication.

The women Straparola specified as part of the storytelling company present a completely different set of narrative problems. Straparola's ten female storytellers are little more than cardboard cutouts.[19] With first names only, without identifiable family connections, the young women as a group stood for a category, and that was how Straparola treated them. They were "as beautiful as they were good," but goodness per se formed a precious small part of his descriptions. Instead, as individuals they had eyes "like glowing stars," a "fine figure," "blond tresses," a "rounded bosom"; as a group they were young women who were "graceful and amorous" and who had "a fluent tongue." When Straparola claimed that one of the young women had "divine virtues" and that another's worthy thoughts made her always ready to perform virtuous deeds, indeed more so than any other woman anywhere in the world (Proem to first night), one feels that Straparola protests their virtue entirely too much.

For men of the eminence that Straparola drew into his frametale there were two relevant kinds of social gatherings in the mid-1500s. One was a courtly gathering at which men and women of high rank met for evenings of music, dance, storytelling, conversation, and refreshment. Everyone present was a known quantity; everyone's relationships by marriage or birth were clearly delineated and socially unambiguous. In his frametale Straparola provides exactly that social network for Ottaviano Maria's daughter, Signora Lucrezia, and the two venerable matrons, with their noble blood—Signora Chiara, the wife of Girolamo Guidiccione, a gentleman of Ferrara, and Signora Veronica, widow of Santo Orbat, whose Crema family was both old and noble (Proem). We can imagine the way these matrons looked from Ambrogio de Predis's portrait of Queen Bianca Maria Sforza, Titian's portrait of Isabella d'Este, or Tintoretto's group portrait of the men and women of the Soranzo family. Those women, their bosoms modestly covered, wore ermine, silk, velvet, and jewels, the unmistakable marks of their elevated class.[20] Their frametale silence accords completely with the maxim current in Venice from the fifteenth century onward that "an eloquent woman is never chaste" (*nullam eloquentem esse castam*) (Labalme 1980, 139, 150n43). This proverb, a likely reference to the literary gifts developed by courtesans, provides yet another distinctive mark separating the three *signore* from Straparola's ten storytelling *damigelle*.

A second kind of social gathering would have included the same men, but the women present would have been vastly different. Rather than the unexceptionably virtuous daughters or wives of known families, the female presence would have consisted of attractive girls and young women, daughters of artisans, shopkeepers, or formerly respectable but now poor citizens. They would all have had the sparkling eyes, rounded bosoms, and blond or reddish hair that prepared goodlooking girls to compete in the marketplace of the Venetian courtesan. These women attracted the attention of prominent men, the money of wealthy patrons, and the paintbrush of Venetian painters. At the very end of his life, even the chaste Giovanni Bellini couldn't resist painting one of them, a redhaired and naked young woman inspecting her coiffure in a mirror. Francesco d'Ubertini (1494–1557) painted an undated sybil, round breasts fully displayed; Giorgione did a *Laura* in 1506; and Titian painted a series of highly sought after beauties, such as *Girl in a Fur Coat* (1535) and *Violante* (1510/15).[21] Any one of these gorgeous women, all portrayed with youthfully and clearly revealed swelling breasts, could have served as a model for the ten young women at Straparola's "Murano" storytelling sessions. Unlike Signora Chiara and Signora Veronica, Straparola gave them no familial resumes. It is precisely the fact that he described them in purely visual terms that suggests to me that they were courtesans like those he would have seen in their easily identifiable dress on Venice's streets and canals.

A courtesan's beauty was augmented by education and accomplishments, as was the case with the young women in Straparola's frametale. Alteria, for instance, played the viol beautifully. Such young women needed to be able to display "beauty, style, good judgment, and proficiency in many skills," in the 1580 words of the successful Venetian courtesan Veronica Franco (Rosenthal 1998, 39). Despite their social talents, courtesans' profitable professional life was relatively brief—from about the age of fifteen until their faces were no longer fresh, after which they would have to sell their bodies to an ever lower social clientele until they were reduced to lurking on the street for customers (Rosenthal 1998, 39–40). Significantly, not one of the ten young women attempts to decipher Bishop Casale's enigma about a unicorn (night 13, story 1), a beast whose chief characteristic was its ability to detect and respond to virginity.

Gatherings that included eminent men and available women might have been augmented by a couple of quick-tongued wags to inspire laughter and by someone of wealth to pick up the tab, someone perhaps like the merchant Ferier Beltramo. On the other hand, by remarking that Ottaviano Maria had left Lodi with jewels, Straparola implied a Sforza payer for thirteen nights' suppers.

Straparola undoubtedly knew, or at least knew of, both kinds of gatherings—the exclusively aristocratic one that was open only to well-placed men and women and the mixed one of nobles, merchants, quick-tongued punsters, and courtesans. If, as I surmise, Straparola was the creative intellect behind a workaday wit in Venice or on the mainland, he would certainly have been well acquainted with courtesans. On the other hand, Straparola's streetwise readers would have immediately known that the two worlds of women described here—the three well-married signoras two of whom were widowed and the first-name-only young women—would never have coexisted night after night for story-telling or any other social purpose. The literary consequence was that Straparola, drawing on a hallowed Boccaccian convention, applied stereotypical descriptions to make each of the pretty storytelling young women into a cynosure of beauty and virtue. A neat solution to an otherwise insoluble mix.

This interpretation of the people present in the *Pleasant Nights* is supported by the curious fact that the named men and the three signoras—whatever kinds of stories they "told"[22]—maintained strict pro-priety in the enigmas they posed, while the ten beautiful young women mouthed ambiguously obscene verses, something Castiglione had iden-tified two decades earlier as characteristic of nonvirtuous women. One example among many was Alteria's enigma, a versified riddle, the sur-face meaning of which referred to sexual intercourse, which "gave the men a lot to talk about" (night 8, story 4). The presiding and highly respectable signora often rebuked the beautiful young women for such indecency. Perhaps Straparola himself had experienced the tenor of courtesans' ways with words that could make men blush, as Castiglione put it succinctly (1903, 143–44). He certainly incorporated such a way with words into the sexual ambiguities of the enigmas presented by his young beauties. In any case, the signora never had to rebuke any of the men for their enigmas, because theirs were always unambiguously moral. Indeed, Antonio Molino's enigma was praised for not being lewd (night 5, story 3), a propriety maintained in Benedetto Trevigiano's enigma in the next story on the same night.

In terms of actual storytelling, Straparola had arranged the order in which storytellers were called on rather mechanically by dividing the young women into two groups of five. The first set consisted of Lau-retta, Alteria, Cateruzza, Eritrea, and Arianna; the second of Isabella, Fiordiana, Lionora, Lodovica, and Vicenza. One set or the other was designated to tell each session's stories, despite the elaborate arrange-ments that had been worked out in the Proem for pulling names from a golden vase.

Straparola's frametale storytelling was not completely automatic, however. On night 2, faced with a glaring psychological incompatibil-ity between the designated storyteller and the tale that came next in his pile of narratives, he abruptly changed the storyteller. In fact, on that night, because two of his five stories couldn't be convincingly told by a woman, he had the designated storytellers bow out in favor of a male storyteller, Antonio Molino. The tale Molino told, a completely masculine tale both emotionally and psychologically, was about Filenio Sisterno, a student in Bologna, who was tricked by three pretty ladies, on whom he took mortifying revenge:

At a dance, Filenio declared his unending love to three married ladies one after the other. Each maintained honor and modesty by not responding, but when they compared notes, they decided to pay him back. Instead of sexual satisfaction, he met in turn thorns, a trap door, and a sleeping potion. As revenge, he arranged a feast for the three women's husbands, in the course of which he decoyed their wives into a small sideroom and made them undress before him by threatening their lives. Then with their faces covered, he exhibited their nether parts to their husbands and also showed them the ladies' clothing and jewels, which the husbands thought they recognized. Filenio feasted with the husbands, but the ladies returned to their homes, put their fine clothes away, and when their husbands returned, pretended to have been sewing all evening.

The ladies present, including the presiding signora, found Filenio's trick both revolting and indecent, although they eventually decided that the ladies' cruel tricks on the student justified his vendetta.

Excusing one of his young women from telling an impossibly male-oriented tale was not Straparola's only accommodation to his fictive young women's fictive feelings. After the ugly story of Filenio Sisterno, Lionora acknowledged that Messer Molino's tale, although she personally found it indecent, was pleasing to the gentlemen. She would therefore tell one equally pleasing to the ladies. Her story mocked men by creating a spectacle of Carlo da Rimini embracing cauldrons and kettles in the besotted belief that they were his beloved's body (night 2, story 3). There followed Signor Benedetto's story of the devil's disastrous marriage to Silvia Balastro (night 2, story 4), which bitterly denounced women for frivolity, bad judgment, and unbridled lust. Signor Benedetto Trivigiano took over the storytelling of this misogynistic tale, in which:

Silvia's peevish humors and insatiable desires drove her demonic husband away from her and into the body of the Duke of Malfi, where he remained until Silvia's impending arrival made him flee.

The men laughed at the story but the women took no pleasure in it. Berating Signor Benedetto, Vicenza said that she herself would propound a story for his edification. In it an amorous Paduan lusted after a peasant's beautiful and virtuous wife. She confided in her husband, who instructed her to allow the lover to visit her one evening, while he was absent. When her husband returned "unexpectedly," the lover hid in a sack, which the peasant dragged outdoors and beat with a cudgel to pay him, a city fellow, back for trying to seduce his wife.

On the fifth night, Straparola once again had two of the female storytellers, Lauretta and Arianna, relinquish their slots to the same two men, Antonio Molino and Benedetto Trivigiano, who again served as Straparola's mouthpieces for stories with a decidedly male cast. In both cases Zoan reproduced dialect in a man's voice. The first was Signor Molino's telling of the story of Zambò (night 5, story 3) in the dialect of Bergamo, to the first part of which I referred in Chapter 3. The story's continuation took place in Rome, where

Zambò took work with Messer Ambros dal Mul. When Messer Ambros suddenly died, Zambò married his widow, Madonna Felicetta. At first he treated her well, but then he began to refuse her permission to buy new clothing and, when she objected, he beat her brutally. This went on until Felicetta was reduced to shaking with fear whenever she heard him returning home.

Eventually Zambò got his just desserts, drowned in the Tiber along with his two revolting brothers. Antonio Molino's telling of Zambò's story betrayed a vicious conjugal violence that no woman would be likely to incorporate into a story she told, even though Zambò's murder and disposal in the Tiber pleased the ladies enormously and kept them laughing and talking about it (night 5, story 3).

The second dialect tale was told by Benedetto Trivigiano in a rustic Paduan dialect (conclusion of night 5, story 3) that Straparola could have learned as an adult. The story itself, of a clever deceiver, was more merry than misogynistic (night 5, story 4). According to Alfredo Stussi, Straparola was better at Paduan than he was with literary Tuscan, for which his explanation is that Straparola might have decided that it wasn't worth the time it would take to edit his book, whose novelty was more important than its linguistic perfection (Stussi 1989, 212). Given the popularity of Il Ruzante's Paduan dramas, a tale told in Paduan can be understood as was yet another canny inclusion in Straparola's compendium of genres and styles.

In a departure from the frametale's practice, the presiding signora, who had not told any story before this, told the final story of the fifth night. Hers was a moral tale about the changes that age makes to the life of a libidinous woman. After the obligatory enigma, a feast followed with dance and song. The fifth and final night of Book 1 ended with the signora asking the Signor Ambassador Gregorio Casale to return to the redoubt according to the custom that had been established (night 5, story 5). The very fact that the signora told the concluding tale of Book 1 signaled a caesura and suggests that Straparola knew ahead of time that the conclusion of her tale would mark the end of the collection until he had the time to write and the money to produce the stories of Book 2.

Adding Songs and Enigmas

It is easy to visualize the next stage in Straparola's creation of the *Pleasant Nights*. On one side of his writing table his stories were stacked, each embedded in the frametale. Straparola had already composed an Introduction, in which he had set out the who, what, when, where, and how of each night's ceremonious progress. But he needed to interleave the songs that initiated each night's festivities and the enigmas that closed each story. For these he may well have turned to songs and enigmas he had composed over the years for the use of his patron, or perhaps he drew them from the popular press. Some of Straparola's enigmas (night 11, story 4; night 7, story 1; night 10, story 4; night 12, story 3) bear a striking resemblance to ones in printed enigma collections, such as Risoluto's *Sonetti* of 1547, while others from Book 2 can be traced to the 1552 *Accademia d'enigmi*. Clearly Straparola was busily borrowing from books (Rua 1890a, 140–51, esp. 148–49). Whatever their ultimate source, the enigmas in Straparola's books were prized in and of themselves: in 1679 Gabriel Sculteti Onghero gathered 51 of his enigmas with their expositions and had the Leipzig publisher "Hans Colero" print them as *Degli spiriti generosi. Passatempo Toscano, ciò è ingegniosi enimmi di M. Giovan Francesco Straparola da Caravaggio.*

Straparola probably worked his way through nights 1 to 5 methodically. At the end of the Proem to the first night, he would have slotted in a song, then have peeled the first story off the top of the stack. On its last page, he would have written in fitting comments and added an enigma. He would have needed to compose a fictive exposition, put it into the mouth of one of the listeners, or—if he allowed none of the listeners to attempt to unravel the enigmatic riddle—into the mouth of the story's teller. Now he would have been ready to add a few sentences to introduce the next storyteller. At that point, the process would begin again: introductory words, story, enigma in fictionalized setting, exposition of the enigma, introductory words, and so on until he'd finished the night's stories. At that point he could conclude with notations about the evening's closing moments: escorted to the landing-place by the flare of torches (first night), dismissed by the signora as the rosy tints of morning appeared in the eastern skies (second night), ordered to depart as the morning star shone in the brightening dawn (third night), required without fail to return the following evening as the morning cock crowed (fourth night), and, as the reddening light of dawn began to appear, begged to return the next evening (fifth night). The second night provides as good an example as any of Straparola's style, method, and frametale language:

Phoebus already had his gilded wheels in the briny waves of the Indian (sic) Ocean and his rays no longer illuminated the earth, and his horned sister everywhere ruled the dark shadows with her clear light and the pretty sparkling stars had already defined the sky with their light, when the courteous and honorable company returned to their usual place to tell stories.

(Aveva già Febo le dorate rote nelle salse onde dell'Indiano mare, ed e'suoi raggi non davano più splendore alla terra, e la sua cornuta sorella le oscure tenebre con la sua chiara luce signoreggiava per tutto e le vaghe e scintilanti stelle avevano già il cielo del suo lume depinto, quando l'onesta e orrevole compagnia al luogo solito a favoleggiare si ridusse.)

The signora directed Benedetto Trivigiano to put the names of the five "damigelle" who hadn't told stories on the previous day into the golden vase, and then to pull them out one after the other to establish the evening's narrative order. That done, Straparola had the flutes sound to begin the girls' and the gentlemen's dance, in which the worthy signoras did not join—another sign of their separateness. After that, everyone sat down. Then the girls praised the signora in a sweet and lovely (*amorosa*) canzone, whose lines rhymed in the schema a-b-b-c-c-d-d-a-d-e-e.

The song concluded, Isabella undertook to tell the first story of the second night, which Straparola had already headed with a content description:

Galeotto King of Anglia had a son born a pig, who got married three times, and after having doffed the pig pelt and having become a superbly handsome youth, was called King Pig.

(Galeotto re di Anglia ha uno figliulo nato porco, il quale tre volte si marita, e posta giù la pelle porcina e divenuto un bellissimo giovane, fu chiamato re Porco.)

"Isabella" addressed the ladies (*graziose donne*), remarking as "she" began the story, that a thousand years of thanks to his creator for not making a man (*uomo*) a beast (*animale brutto*) would be an insufficient expression of gratitude. That, she continued, called to mind something that had happened in their own day (*una favola a' tempi nostri*). There followed the story of "Prince Pig." At its conclusion, Straparola added a brief reprise:

The tale told by Isabella provoked laughter at the end, when the men and the ladies (*donne*) were highly amused at milord the pig all befouled, who caressed his beloved wife.

(Era già ridotta al suo termine la favola da Issabella (sic) raccontata, quando gli uomini de le donner sommamente si ridevono de messer lo porco tutto inlordato che accareciava la sua diletta moglie.)

Signora Lucrezia then requested Isabella to pose her enigma, which she did with a smile, beginning

I'd like you to give me, o my lord,
That which you never had nor ever will.

(Vorrei che tu mi desti, o mio signore,
quel che non hai né sei per aver mai.)

No one could solve her ingenious enigma, and so the wise (*la prudente*) Isabella had to expound it herself: a man gives a woman a husband when he marries her, and yet a husband is something a man does not nor ever will have. The assembled company greeted the resolution of her enigma with pleasure, after which Fiordiana, although she was supposed to go next, stood and suggested that "our Molino" amuse the company with one of his *facetiae*, because, she added, "simple ladies, it is better to have the needle in one's hand than to tell stories" (*semplici donne, starebbe meglio l'aco in mano che 'l raccontare le favole*)! Praising Fiordiana for her prudence, Signora Lucrezia, her eyes on Molino, said he should tell a pretty story (*leggiadra favola*). He accepted. The story, that of Filenio Sisterno's sexual mortification of the three ladies who had not succumbed to his offers of lovemaking, was not pretty at all. Straparola had the girls (*damigelle*) and Signora Lucrezia object to it, initially at least, after Molino posed his enigma and provided its exposition. Then came the lead-in to the third story of the second night.

The invariant succession of introductions, stories, enigmas, and expositions confirm the hypothesis that Straparola was working according to a pattern that he implemented *after* he had assembled the stories themselves. If he had incorporated these elements at the time at which he assembled the stories, there would have been occasional narrative friction between the story told and the chosen narrator. But that did not happen, because Straparola had first chosen the stories, and had then tampered with the choice of narrators to assure a good fit between the two.

Once Straparola had slotted all five nights' stories into his fictive frametale, he had completed the first part of his task. Never mind that in its final form there was little cohesion in the frametale and minimal characterization of the fictive narrators. The enigmas that followed each tale were equally unrelated to the stories that preceded them, which also confirms the likelihood that they were added after Straparola completed the stories. Whatever the manuscript's faults, Book 1 was finished.

Permission to Publish and the Privilege

Although Straparola had concluded the writing phase of Book 1, imperfect though it was, there was still one more step to be taken. In Venice it was legally required to secure permission to publish, a process that required that a manuscript be examined for doctrinal error, moral lapse, political content, or diplomatic effect (Grendler 1977, 151–54). It was a formality that was often ignored. But if Straparola also wished to have protection against another person's printing and selling his stories out from under him, obtaining a privilege was absolutely essential. It was this step that would enable Straparola to be certain of harvesting the financial fruit of his labors, the phrase so often used in this connection (Richardson 1999, 78). Straparola took no chances: he submitted his manuscript to the Venetian authorities and was granted a privilege on 8 March 1550—not unanimously, however, for five members of the council voted against the book. In the surviving document, one can read that two people received copyrights on that day that granted each a ten-year right to exclusive publication of his book. It further specified that nobody else, without his permission, was allowed to print, or have printed, or sell the named book in any place "in our domain," that is, Venice and the Veneto, for the next ten years, under pain of forfeiting all copies of the illegally produced book and of paying a fine of 100 ducats, which would be divided equally among the accuser, the magistrate who carried out the process, and the Arsenal. For his part, the author who received the privilege was obligated to observe the laws relating to printing and publishing.[23]

The privilege date provides a point of reference for dating the completion of Book 1.[24] By this I mean that the granting of a privilege did not follow instantaneously on presentation of a finished manuscript. Consequently, one may reasonably conclude that Straparola finished the stories of Book 1 sometime in January or February 1550. Counting backward from the completion date, we may further imagine that nights 1–5 were composed in the summer and fall of 1549, which returns us to the anachronistic heat of the January Carneval.

The Letter to Readers of the *Piacevoli Notti*

On opening the book, after the title page, the first text readers saw was a letter to the ladies by "Orpheo dalla Carta." No one by that name is known to have existed in the Venice of Straparola's day. To date three identities have been suggested for "Orpheo." Giuseppe Rua holds him to be Straparola's "editore" (1890a, 127n1). In his article, "Danza, Paolo e Prospero" in the monumental 1997 reference work, *Dizionario dei tipographi e degli editori italiani*, Steno Zanandrea associates him with the Danza family (cited in Pirovano 2002, n2). Donato Pirovano refines that identification to his being Straparola's "finanziatore/promotore" (2000, 543–45).

The letter is important because it provides the basis for the erroneous belief that Straparola simply set down what he'd heard at a thirteen-night Murano gathering for "the pleasure of those who might always rely on him for his service to them." An author's pretended reticence was of course a common trope in the Renaissance and for centuries thereafter. Heaven forfend that he'd done so to gratify his pride or to make money! In Straparola's case, the pretense is not even carried through. The colophon recorded for all the world to see that the book was printed "ad instanza dall'autore," at the author's behest.

The very name "Orpheo" suggests additional, perhaps wholly other possibilities, for it smacks of a pseudonym of the sort used by literary academy members in the 1550s. Anton Francesco Doni did not list an "Orfeo" among academy members in Venice and the Veneto (Doni 1557, 277–284), but his list is unlikely to be complete. Chaffing himself, or being chaffed by someone else, "Orpheo" may refer to a latter-day undertaking in which Straparola did not lead Eurydice from the underworld, but exited from his hellish travails with a sheet of paper (*carta*). But did Straparola's pen produce these paragraphs?

It is unlikely that Straparola himself wrote the letter to readers, since he himself, unlike "Orpheo," surely would not have forgotten that he had two male storytellers among his narrators. Furthermore, "Orpheo dalla Carta"'s description of the author as the "ingegnoso messer Gioanfrancesco Straparola da Caravaggio" is pure tongue-in-cheek touting, something that someone who had a financial interest in the book's success would have wished to emphasize, and that person would have been, beyond Straparola himself, Comin da Trino, who could only have hoped to land more business by having his author sell out all copies of the first printing. The dissociation of the printer from the stories' low style ("Appresso di cio uoi non risguardarete il basso . . ." (Straparola 1551, A iil^r; also 1555) strongly suggests Comin da Trino, or someone deputized by him, as the author of the letter to the readers.

Let us also remember that Straparola had called himself "Zoan" on the title pages of his youthful production, the *Opera nova*, and that he was "Zuan" in the wording of the 1550 privilege. But in "dalla Carta"'s letter to the ladies, Straparola appears as Gioanfrancesco. That is, the "John" part of his name is neither "Giovan" nor "Giovanni," Tuscan equivalents of his Lombard Zoan. Instead he is named "Gioan," a Tuscanized spelling of "Zoan" that also suggests a speaking acquaintance between Straparola and the person writing the address to the ladies.

The Printing

Brian Richardson's *Printing, Writers, and Readers in Renaissance Italy* (1999) provides an invaluable source of information about Venetian authorship, privileges, financing, print, and publishing in the late 1400s and throughout the 1500s. Richardson documents the fact that fifteenth- and sixteenth-century authors often financed part or all of the printing costs, so that they could share in or enjoy all the profits from the sale of their books (69–76). The fact that Straparola's privilege appeared in his own name is therefore probable evidence that Straparola financed some or all the production costs for *Pleasant Nights*.

Several possibilities existed for shared investment in book production. Because the privilege mentions only Straparola's name, his most likely cofinancing would have been a relatively simple two-part package. Straparola might, for example, have put together a package that consisted of his own resources augmented by investment from a bookseller who would take on his books as a promising bit of merchandise. Once financial arrangements were organized, Straparola would have been ready to order paper, a costly component in the mid-1500s (Lowry 1992, 365), to ascertain that good quality ink would be used, and to discuss the book's typeface. Straparola and Comin da Trino eventually settled on an italic typeface, and with that detail decided, Straparola would have handed over the manuscript.

During the ten months between the 8 March 1550 privilege and the 3 January 1551 conclusion of printing Comin da Trino set type and printed the *Pleasant Nights*. Since Straparola's stories for Book 1 would eventually consist of some 23 sheets folded into small octavos, theoretically 500–1000 copies of the book could have been printed in about twenty-three workdays, or faster if speed was the main objective. That didn't happen—the printing was only completed early the following January. Perhaps Straparola spent part of that time trying to negotiate a better deal with another printer or working out the best price he could arrange with paper and ink suppliers, for after 450 years the paper of *Pleasant Nights* remains supple and the ink crisply clear. Or perhaps Comin da Trino simply wanted to wait until the beginning of Carneval to bring out a book that ostensibly took place at that time.

The date Comin da Trino finished printing Book 1, 3 January 1551, initiated a different kind of negotiating, for if Straparola had paid for part or all of the printing costs, then he would also have been responsible for the commercial distribution of the books. He undoubtedly gave some as gifts to individuals among whom he hoped to find a new patron; the rest were commercially salable at the bookshop at the sign of Saint Alvise, as the title page informs us.

It is likely, therefore, that Straparola spent the weeks and months after 3 January 1551 personally overseeing distribution of books to the bookseller at the sign of Saint Alvise.

Sales

Straparola and Comin da Trino tested the waters cautiously. They did so not once, but twice. That is, Comin da Trino finished printing the first five nights' stories in early January 1551 (by the modern calendar) as a small octavo, half the size of a twentieth-first-century paperback. On the title page stood not his own name, but the fictional "Orpheo dalla Carta."[25]

The first printing sold well, and in the same year Comin da Trino's journeymen set type and printed the first five nights' stories a second time. This time the sheets were placed at a bookseller at Saint Luke at the sign of the Diamond (A San Luca al Segno del diamante), with whom Comin da Trino often worked. Just off the Grand Canal, the Campo San Luca was a good neighborhood: from there, one could look across the canal of San Luca to the elegant Gothic palace of the Corner Contarini, built a century before. (In the end, the bookshop at the sign of the Diamond carried only the second printing, with all other printings of Book 1 sold at the sign of Saint Alvise.)

Inevitably the question arises why *Pleasant Nights* appeared as it did. Why did Book 1 end with no indication about when the sixth night's taletelling would commence? Other authors often promised readers that they'd produce a sequel or continuation if and when their books had sold out and begged readers not to lend out their books to friends and acquaintances, because lending undermined sales.

Two explanations for the doubled printing of Book 1 seem possible. The first is that Straparola may not have been either willing or able to shoulder the large expenditure required (for paper, ink, inkballs, a printer, and his assistant) to publish the entire collection at one time. Fiscal prudence dictated caution (publishing the first five nights on their own). But personal optimism probably led Straparola to assume that his stories *would* sell, that he would be able to continue the process of assembling stories and producing a fictive frametale within a relatively short period of time, and that he would bring the subsequent nights' tales to the market. In the end, however, two years passed before Book 2 was printed.

Book 2: The Contents and Composition

It was probably sometime in early or late spring 1552 that Straparola began to compose the stories of Book 2, beginning with the sixth night. He followed the same composition pattern as for the first five nights, that is, first assembling the stories, then adding enigmas and songs, and finally concocting an appropriate frametale. The tone had changed, however. On the sixth night Straparola presented four stories about women's bodies, two of them brutally coarse. For one of them, an account of three nuns' genito-urinary dexterity (night 6, story 4), he removed the designated storyteller Lauretta and substituted Antonio Bembo, since this was hardly an appropriate tale for a young woman of reputed beauty and virtue to tell. After that, Straparola seems to have been at a loss for a story to complete the sixth night's storytelling. Casting about for ideas, he made a choice that was decisive for the contents of Book 2 and colored this volume very differently from the first one. His eyes fell on a copy of Morlini's Latin *Novellae*, and leafing through it he chose a tale about a thief in a fig tree, the pragmatic moral of which was that stones work better than incantations if you want to rout a marauder. Except for the fig thief story, the sixth night's tales had been remarkably vulgar, so much so that the *Pleasant Nights* English translator W. G. Waters resorted to French for lengthy passages. Their rank bawdiness inspired Straparola to a rare intratextual comment at the sixth evening's conclusion, when he had the storyteller Eritrea hark back to two similarly provocative stories Cateruzza had told earlier.

Straparola continued writing into the summer through the seventh, eighth, ninth, and tenth nights, carelessly and anachronistically putting the sights and sounds of summer—flitting fireflies (night 8, introduction), screeching grasshoppers (night 9, story 5), and thick-leaved trees (night 10, introduction)—into his descriptions of the frametale midwinter Carneval celebration.[26]

It was very likely in late summer or early autumn 1552 that Straparola composed his masterpiece, the story of Costantino Fortunato. Afterward, something—we'll probably never know what—stopped Straparola in his tracks. Perhaps he was incapacitated by illness. In any case, after "Costantino and his Cat" Straparola stepped back from the collection and seems to have accepted help from someone else to complete Book 2. At that point he would have had a pile of 26 stories, but no enigmas, no songs, and no frametale. All that had to be supplied, and was supplied by someone else altogether. Perhaps it was a friend, perhaps an editor in Comin da Trino's employ, who stepped in hastily and translated and assembled stories one after another (except for one) from a single source, Morlini's *Novellae*.

In the first ten nights, Straparola had grouped stories more or less thematically. Under the new editor, all semblance of narrative order was gone. Whoever completed Straparola's book lifted Morlini's stories at random: Morlini's tale 7 was followed by 36, then came 26, 30, 71, and 27.

The helper was also careless in ways Straparola had not been, and the change is evident. For instance, he repeated the enigma for night 6, story 1 after night 8, story 3. The enigmas' rhyme pattern continued the ababab cc scheme familiar from Book 1. In a deeper sense the stories' enigmas remained consistent with those of Book 1; like Straparola, the new frametale organizer kept lewd enigmas out of the mouths of the three noble signoras and their honorable male guests, while leaving obscene ones for the mouths of the beautiful "damigelle." A case in point is the purity of the enigmas of Antonio Molino. That of night 7, story 2 was as explicitly acceptable to the signora as his enigma of night 5, story 3 had been, as she explicitly noted in the frametale.

With the introductory songs, however, the assistant betrayed his participation to a greater extent. Each of Book 1's sung entertainments had been a *canzone*, whose rhyme schemes Straparola artfully enhanced one after the other. Consider them in chronological order:

night 1	abbcddcaee
night 2	abbccddadee
night 3	abbacdedcdff
night 4	abccbadeeddff
night 5	abbcaddcceefgfg

The increases in length and complexity in each *canzone* occurred with reference to the preceding one, with an evident internal coherence that reveals literary intention. My hypothesis—that someone other than Straparola provided the frametale apparatus for all of Book 2—is corroborated by the complete absence of the tightly structured verse patterning Straparola had established in Book 1.[27]

In the eight nights of Book 2's introductory songs there are four canzones and four madrigals, the latter a form alien to Book 1. Furthermore, in Book 2 no conscious patterning emerges from the structures of the canzone and madrigals, whether one considers them as a whole, or as two individual groups.

night 6	madrigal	abbcddcaee
night 7	canzone	abbcdedffecc
night 8	madrigal	abbcddcee (note also the flawed rhyme scheme, which lacks a second "a")
night 9	canzone	abbcdcdefeff
night 10	canzone	abbacdedceffgg
night 11	madrigal	abbcadcaddee
night 12	madrigal	abbcdecdeaff
night 13	canzone	abbcdedceeaff

Content, too, distinguished the last of the introductory evening songs from Straparola's canzone in Book 1, for the canzone of night 13 incorporated phrases from or reminiscent of Petrarch, Bembo, Boccaccio, and Ariosto (Straparola 2000, 2: 730n1–5), marks consistent with a showy display of learning by an ambitious young editor.

In the frametale itself glaring errors suddenly appeared of the sort that would have been made by someone unfamiliar with the preceding stories and frametale. Narrators changed in midcourse, with Alteria suddenly slotted into Lauretta's place (night 8, story 4); where Lodovica should have told a tale on the ninth night, someone mistakenly inserted an unknown and unidentified character named "Diana," who appeared again on the eleventh night and then evaporated when Lodovica suddenly reappeared on the twelfth night.

Another kind of break appeared at the beginning of night 13, not just the obvious fact that having thirteen storytellers burst the regularity of Straparola's five-stories-per-night pattern on the thirteenth and final night of storytelling, but the very order of storytelling. For twelve nights, as it had been decreed on the first night, storytellers took their turn in an order set by pulling names from a golden urn. On the thirteenth night, it was not blind chance but known hierarchy that determined order. The ambassador, Signor Casale, went first. Then storytelling continued in descending order with Signora Lucrezia, Signor Pietro Bembo, Signora Veronica, Signor Bernardo Capello, Signora Chiara, Signor Beltramo, Lauretta, Signor Antonio Molino, Cateruzza, Signor Benedetto Trivigiano, Isabella, and finally Vicenza taking a turn. Two regular storytellers, Lionora and Fiordiana, disappeared from the final night, even though Antonio Bembo had been enamored of Fiordiana in the Proem to the first night, and Straparola had made a feeble attempt to provide frametale interest by halfheartedly chronicling their budding romance.

The introductions to storytelling for both nights 12 and 13 also differed from preceding introductions by similarly giving importance to class. In Book 1's Proem, "rank" had appeared glancingly ("having seated themselves according to rank" / *messisi tutti a sedere secondo i gradi loro*), and had then faded from frametale utterances during the next ten nights. On night 12 the hierarchical concept returned. Instead of acknowledging the guests' "gradi" (rank) in descriptive terms, however, the modified authorial voice wrote prescriptively of their "ordini" (class). And even though the frametale terminology of night 13 repeated that of night 1 ("gradi"), the lengthy storytelling episode itself enacted and expressed the fixity of social hierarchy, which resulted in the exclusion of several of the frametale's customary storytellers.

A further distinction separated the thirteenth night from those preceding it. On this night alone, when the narrators were arranged in hierarchically descending order, particular care was taken to match stories with the narrators who told them. That means that on this night, the narrators must have been chosen first and then stories chosen to suit the narrators.

Surprisingly, the errors that had plagued whoever worked on nights 11 and 12 disappeared on night 13. This bespeaks a second editorial fracture between nights 12 and 13 in addition to the one that occurred after "Costantino and His Cat" (night 11, story 1).

In tone the frametale of Book 2 also differed significantly from that of Book 1 in ways that are consistent with a self-advertising familiarity with the great world of Venetian letters. For example, whoever composed the frametale in Book 2 intimated personal knowledge of the well-known versifier Bernardo Capello (1498–1565) by referring to his seriousness *(ogni suo grave pensiero*, night 13, story 4). Still literarily active at the time of Straparola's composition, Capello published his *Rime* five years after *Pleasant Nights* appeared (Richardson 1994, 2;

Pirovano in Straparola 2000, 1: 9n6). Similarly, personal information was slipped in about the gambling of Antonio Bembo, Pietro Bembo's cousin (*che del giuoco assai si dilettava*, night 13, story 5) and about the merry look of the Treviso merchant Ferier Beltramo (*ma con gioconda faccia a letizia inclinata*, night 13, story 6). These are observations the more reserved Straparola had not allowed himself. Similar asides characterize Signora Lucrezia Sforza's two companions. In the Proem Straparola had identified Signora Chiara only as the wife of Girolamo Guidiccione from Ferrara, but the person who composed the frametale of Book 2 observed that she was rather short (*percioché era picciola*, night 13, story 5) and that she was a woman who thought no evil (night 13, story 6).

Finally, on the thirteenth evening, the storytelling of the *Pleasant Nights* closed for good. The next day would be the first day of Lent, and so the men departed to their homes, the women remained with the signora, and conversation, dances, music, and stories were put aside.

The end of *Pleasant Nights* did not end the preparation of the manuscript, however. Some people, whether through envy or malice, had accused Straparola of stealing stories from others. He rejected the charge vigorously and, "to speak the truth" acknowledged that the stories were not his, after all, but those of the ten "damigelle." That done, he dated his address to his female readers the first of September 1553.

Straparola or perhaps his bookseller at San Bortholomeo wanted one last thing—a portrait of the author. And so a truncated portrait was created, set into a medium-cost frame of concentric oval lines and drapery, and published for all the Venetian reading world to see. It is not curious that the portrait was placed in Book 2 at this point. What's odd is that the portrait remained in Book 2 (during Straparola's lifetime) and was not repositioned in Book 1 for the next printing, where authorial portraits normally appear, both then and now. Both Books 1 and 2 began with an address to the reader, that in Book 1 by the fictive Orfeo dalla Carta, that in Book 2 by Straparola himself. Perhaps we should understand the Book 2 placement of the portrait just before his heartfelt defense of his authorship as a visual confirmation of his both claimed and disclaimed authorial presence.

The year 1553 is the third significant date for the *Pleasant Nights*, marking the conclusion of the printing of Book 2 and the beginning of its distribution and sales. Let us assume that Comin da Trino's printer, aided by an apprentice, printed at the rate of 1,000–1,500 sheets per day

for Book 2, a routine rate in 1500s Venice (Richardson 1999 24). The
first printing of Book 2, with 20 sheets, was a little shorter than Book
1, which means that a print run of 1,000–1,500 copies could have
been completed in twenty working days. But with Comin da Trino's
establishment "probably the most active in this period in Venice," any
number of interruptions might have taken place (Donvito 1997, 310–11).
In any case, Straparola dated his address to his readers 1 September 1553,
and the book appeared in the same calendar year as it then existed, that
is, any time up to the end of February 1554, but very probably a bit
earlier, so that it would appear toward the beginning of Carneval, as
had Book 1.

For the first printing of Book 2, Straparola—or Comin da Trino—
chose a different bookseller, whose shop was on the western edge of
the bookselling center and in the heart of Venice's German-speaking
merchant community. Near the huge and brilliantly frescoed trading
center of the Fondaco dei Tedeschi and close to the Rialto Bridge,
San Bortholomeo (Bartolomeo in modern spelling) was extremely well
placed to reach a broad variety of potential buyers.

Even though less than two years had passed between the second
printing of Book 1 and the first printing of Book 2, it was a long time in
the life of a man nearing seventy. Straparola survived to see Book 2's
nights 6–13 published in 1553, a second printing in 1554, and additional
printings of Book 1 in 1555, but probably not the 1556 printing.

Comin da Trino interrupted the 1555 printing even as his workers
were printing the first set of sheets and hanging them up to dry. Something made him decide to change the title page date at that point to
"1556" and "1557." All the fascicles in the 1555 "1556," and "1557" editions
have the same fingerprint and are therefore part of the same print run.
The placement and spacing of the "I" the typesetters added to the
"M.D.LI." to make it "M.D.LII." make it clear that the page was not
overprinted at some time after the initial print run. Neither did anyone
replace the 1555 title page with a 1556 or a 1557 one, because the entire
title page is integral to the sheet folded to make fascicle A. (There is no
telltale tab visible between fascicle A and B.)

Changing the title page date *during* a print run was, to say the least,
an uncommon practice in Renaissance Venice, and it strongly suggests
that Comin da Trino—or someone else—expected that some event was
going to cause this printing of Straparola's book to sell more slowly
than previous printings had done. To keep the sheets of a 1555 printing

from looking last year's book when they lay on the bookseller's shelf in 1557, Comin's printers changed the date to "M.D.LI." and "M.D.LII."

In searching for reasons for the date change, we should concentrate not on long-term conditions, such as an economic downturn and a slowdown in book purchasing, but on a sudden event. Of those, two possibilities suggest themselves. The designated bookseller's premises could have been destroyed, but that obviously didn't happen because the bookseller "at the sign of S. Alvise" remained on the altered title page. Far more likely is the author's death. He may have fallen to the devastating plague of 1555–56, or a chronic disorder may have felled him on the very day that—print having been set anew—the first sheet of the third edition of Book 1 of his *Piacevoli Notti* began to be stamped.

We can imagine the scene. Surprise, consternation, the owner of the bookshop at Sant'Alvise suddenly appearing, hastily conferring with Comin da Trino, perhaps pointing out that without Straparola's personal promotion sales would slow down, abruptly stopping the presses, adding another "I" to the date and moving the "." to the right. Then the presses with their already inked plates resumed their clanking production.

After the "1555," which is to say also the "1556" and the "1557" printing, the book ceased to be Straparola's. His portrait disappeared from the frontispiece, and printers stopped announcing that the printing had taken place at his behest. His visual and verbal absence from the printing and publishing process after "1557" is as certain an announcement of his death as we are likely to encounter.

Conclusion

Straparola displayed relatively little care for literary excellence as he produced the tales of *Pleasant Nights*. The examples are myriad. There is also abundant evidence throughout the collection that Straparola sent his manuscript to Comin da Trino uncorrected. For example, in "Prince Pig" he named Meldina not when he first introduced her but almost as an afterthought, long after she had entered the story. Livoretto (night 3, story 2) kept *pigs* for the (necessarily Muslim) Sultan of Cairo, something that well-traveled Venetians would have recognized for the factual error it was. Samaritana (night 3, story 3) allegedly disappeared because Biancabella failed to keep her commandment, even though Biancabella had not in fact broken a commandment. He described Alchaia, whom Fortunio murdered for betraying him, as a "worthy and amiable" person (night 3, story 4). He put the quintessentially male tale of sexual gratification and concomitant mortification of two charmingly witless women (night 6, story 1) into the mouth of a female narrator, Alteria, even though in other cases he made his female narrators object to misogynistic plots. This partial listing of Straparola's narrative errors communicates more clearly than any other evidence that he wrote his tales hurriedly and without correction. Straparola's first-draft, error-ridden texts make it obvious that neither he, nor his printer, nor an editor polished his prose for style and accuracy.[28]

Of the public's response to the *Pleasant Nights* we know two things: they bought Book 1 with alacrity, and some reader or readers complained that stories in Book 2 were not Straparola's own but had been stolen from other authors. In a contemporary court of law, Straparola's detractors would handily win any suit brought on the basis of intellectual property. But in a day when Chaucer borrowed Petrarch's Griselda and Shakespeare adopted Boaistuau's translation of Bandello's Romeo and Juliet, different standards affected views on "authorship."[29] Straparola defended "his" stories vigorously in the foreword to the first printing of Book 2 in 1553 and again in 1555. After this, he made no new claims about authorship.

We can only imagine that, at the end of a life devoted to words, Straparola's literary output restored him to a comfortable solvency. He had written a book that appealed to literary tastes that ranged from refined to raunchy: each night's songs addressed "love," the stories told about sex and money, and the enigmas often purveyed either explicit images of or ambiguously phrased references to male sexual arousal.

"Straparola at His Desk" confirms the complex of literary, social, and commercial considerations that constituted popular authorship near the end of the first century of printing. Far from a solitary feat of inspired creativity, the *Pleasant Nights* was something of a trawl through the existing culture. Another way of understanding the book is as a recycling of much that was old and familiar in a form that was novel and appealing. Authorship involved introducing new twists in old tales, and providing settings that were relevant, or even fashionable, without giving offense to important personages. Much was borrowed or even stolen, but it was shaped anew in forms that were currently in demand. So while the tales themselves were entirely fictional in the sense that they related no actual events, the frame was swimming with real people. The frametale of the *Pleasant Nights* often feels modern and relevant, for it communicates an immediacy of the sort we would recognize if a narrator today told his audience, "Jackie Kennedy (or Harold Bloom) told me this one."

5

Straparola's Little Books and
Their Lasting Legacy

IN THE FIRST FIFTY YEARS OF ITS published life the *Pleasant Nights* went through twenty printings. When one considers that it took Boccaccio's admired and beloved *Decameron* fifty years to achieve its first sixteen printings (Waters 1898, 4: 244), the scope of Straparola's success becomes immediately apparent.

The copyright that Straparola held, and that would remain valid until 8 March 1560, protected his financial rights to a book that proved to be a valuable commodity. Its transfer would have been marked by public record, and somewhere documents may still exist that record the passing of copyright from Straparola, who died before it expired, to Comin da Trino, and in 1558 to Domenico Giglio.

When copyright lapsed in 1560 the text of Straparola's tale collection was up for grabs, and the first to grasp it was Francesco Lorenzini, who had come to Venice from Turin, and who immediately published the *Pleasant Nights*. Comin da Trino printed it one last time in 1562, after which various publishers brought it out at intervals of one to three years until 1573. Anton Doni had noted "Straparola da Caravaggio. Cinque notti, primo libro. Libro secondo" (five nights, first book. Second book) in his compendious overview of available books (Doni 1557, 101), which undoubtedly fueled sales for years.

The publishing pace remained remarkably fast during the rest of the sixteenth century, with four hesitant periods—one four-year interval (1586–90), two five-year intervals (1573–78 and 1608–13), and one long seven-year interval (1590–97); during this last period the work was on two papal indexes of forbidden books, something at which the Venetian printer Daniel Zanetti thumbed his nose when he published it in 1597, 1598, and 1601. Zanetto Zanetti (his son?) did the same in 1604 and

1608. Only Alessandro de' Vecchi braved the Zanetti hegemony in these years, printing an edition in 1599.

In terms of untrammeled publication, the first edition of Straparola's *Pleasant Nights* appeared at the last possible moment, just as municipal and church censorship began to muzzle novella and tale collections. Massucio's *Novellae* and Aretino's *Sette salmi* were censored in 1551. The last time that Poggio Bracciolini's *Facetiae* appeared uncensored was 1553. Bandello's *Novelle* were censored on their first appearance in 1554, the *Decameron* in 1557, Firenzuola's *Novelle* in 1562 (Coseriu 1987, 68–69). Straparola couldn't have missed the message communicated by the censorship of Aretino in 1551, in addition to which he might have learned of the objections by a certain "Possevinus S.J." to sordid obscenities in *Pleasant Nights* (reported in Arisius 1741, n.p.). At the time that *Pleasant Nights* was first published, the Inquisition's principal concern had been to locate, identify, and eradicate heretical religious views in printed books, but by the later 1500s it was scrutinizing their moral and political attitudes as well.

Objections like those listed in the preceding paragraph clearly led Straparola to censor his own work. This he did, for example, when he prudently changed night 8, story 3 before the second printing. In profligate Venice it had not perhaps been farfetched to reproduce the old story about a randy priest who tried to save himself by leaping from the bed of his beloved to a niche in the wall, where he stretched out his arms and pretended to be the crucified Christ. His unmistakable erection drew first the gaze and then the sharpened knife of the outraged husband, and the priest fled. Because of the Inquisition's scrutiny, Straparola—or his printer—replaced the bawdy priest with two other stories, one that warned against too much geriatric sex and a second that, true to Venice's lively commercial life, exposed a dishonest merchant. In this way secular scamps took the place of clerical rascals, which was predictive for the editing that continued to alter Straparola's book as the century wore on (see also Rua 1890a, 120).

Another result of general guidelines issued by the Council of Trent (1545–63) in its attempts to reform Catholic personal and institutional behavior was that magic also began to be edited out of Italian tales. The first effects in the *Pleasant Nights* were felt in 1565 in the plots of "Peter the Fool" (night 3, story 1) and "Ortodosio Simeoni and His Flanders Moll" (night 7, story 1). In its efforts to regularize and control

Christian belief and practice, Christian-related words such as "glorioso," "sacro," "divino," and "anima" as well as pagan-tinged vocabulary such as "fortuna" and "fato" were all eventually expunged (Senn 1993, 54). Nonetheless, Straparola's magic and that of his predecessors made it into the consciousness of writers like Andrea Calmo, who in corresponding with a Signora Frondosa in 1552 listed numerous tales of magic, some of which Straparola's restoration tales must have recalled to his memory (Calmo 1580 65ᵛ-67ʳ, esp. 66ᵛ).

Objections such as those to obscenity and magic resulted in the *Pleasant Nights*'s being forbidden by the Parma Index in 1580. In 1590 Pope Sixtus V put "Joannis Francisci Strapparolae (sic) Le piacevoli notte (sic)" along with nearly every other contemporary novella collection onto his Index. In 1596 Clement VIII prohibited it in his Index (Coseriu 1987, 39, 47), and the *Pleasant Nights* was again indexed in 1604 (De Filippis, 1947, 137). The revising process continued decade by decade, so that the content of the *Pleasant Nights* was slowly but continuously recrafted from the mid-1550s to 1608, when it ceased being published in Venice (Senn 1993, 51–54; Pirovano in Straparola 2000, 556–69).

At least one tale from the *Pleasant Nights* entered Italy's chapbook tradition quite soon after its first printing. By 1558 there were two chapbook editions—one an octavo, the other a quarto—of the story of Salardo's unnaturally ingrate wife and adopted son, the book's first tale (Pirovano in Straparola 2000, 810). Presented as a newsworthy "prodigy," its title did not recapitulate the story's contents, as it had done in Straparola's Book 1, but announced the story's facts as though they had just happened (*Copia di un caso notabile intervenuto a un gran gentiluomo genovese . . . cosa molto utile da intender et di gran piacere*). In this way it became part of the day's "news." The story presented so gripping a tale of filial ingratitude and wifely insubordination that it was still appearing as "news" around 1790, under much the same 230-year old title.[1] The question naturally arises whether other stories came onto the market as chapbooks between 1558 and 1613.

As far as magic tales are concerned, those that survived and were collected in the field in the nineteenth century were principally in the forms they took in their Basilean incarnations (Rubini 1998, 225, 238–39n141, 245–46n175). Examples of Straparola's rise tales that appeared in Basile's collection are "Peter the Fool" (night 3, story 1), "The Magic

Doll" (night 5, story 2), and "Costantino and His Cat" (night 11, story 1). These stories lived on reformulated, respectively, as Basile's "Pervonto" (day 1, story 3; Bottigheimer 1993), "The Goose" (day 5, story 1), and "Cagliuso" (day 2, story 4). Straparola's folktale "Three Brothers" (night 7, story 5) expanded itself into Basile's "Five Sons" (day 5, story 7), and "Cesarino" (night 10, story 3) is analogous to Basile's "Merchant's Two Sons" (day 1, story 7). Some of Straparola's restoration tales, such as "Doralice" (night 1, story 4), took a new form in Basile ("The Bear," day 2, story 6). What is remarkable is the fact that there is less apparent direct influence by Straparola on Basile in the 1620s and 1630s than on French fairytale writers 80–90 years later in the 1690s.

Even though municipal and papal prohibitions effectively silenced Straparola's collection after 1613, it was not to be contained. It had gone to France fifty years before.

The *Pleasant Nights* Outside Italy

French publishers wasted no time in adopting the *Pleasant Nights* as their own *Facétieuses nuictes de Straparole*. According to Pierre Jannet, a few of Straparola's stories had already appeared in Lyons by 1553 (Straparola 1857, xii). In 1560 Guillaume Rouille issued Book 1, which Jean Louveau had translated. An Italian-born French bookman, Jean de Larivey, translated Book 2 about ten years after that, and some years later edited Louveau's translation of Book 1. In this form the *Facétieuses nuictes* marched from Lyons north to the print centers of Paris and Rouen, where it was brought out at an astonishing rate of twelve times in eighteen years between 1571 and 1589. But even in France the forbidding reach of the Papal Index stopped its publication under its own name (though not in adaptations by writers like Mme d'Aulnoy) from 1615 until the early 1700s, when Bernard La Monnoie edited one edition and another followed in the Netherlands.

The *Pleasant Nights* emigrated to Spain nearly as fast as to France. After an early appearance, probably in the 1570s,[2] it had a five-year concentration of printings in quick succession: 1578, 1580, 1581, 1582, and 1583.[3] As in Italy, however, Sixtus V's and Clement VIII's Indexes had a chilling effect on its publishing history. A defiant final 1611/1612 printing closed its Spanish history (Senn 1993).

In Germany, where among Italian narratives Boccaccio's stories had pride of place, only three early printings of Straparola's stories are recorded (1575, 1582, 1590), none of which, alas, survives. A late sixteenth-century German taste for the kinds of stories Straparola and his contemporaries published evidently existed, for in 1582 a tale collection devoted largely to *facetiae* was published in Leipzig in Italian, under the title *Passa-tempo de' curiosi*. Two centuries later, when fairy tales were a commercially successful literary product, three publishers brought out Straparola's *Pleasant Nights*. In Vienna I. Alberti was the first, with *Die Nächte des Straparola* in 1791. Berlin presented a north German public with Friedrich Wilhelm Valentin Schmidt's *Märchen des Straparola* as volume 1 in the *Märchen-Saal* of 1817, based on a much expurgated Italian edition of 1608. In Leipzig, Saxony's center of print, A. von Keller produced *Italienischer Novellenschatz* in 1851. In the same period it traveled further north to Denmark for a single printing in 1818, a direct translation of Schmidt's 1817 *Märchen des Straparola*.[4] Among early nineteenth-century bookbuyers prim tastes militated against buying Straparola's *Pleasant Nights* for children, while adults who might buy it for themselves could find far more satisfyingly salacious reading in eighteenth-century French erotica.

The *Pleasant Nights* never really caught on in England. There only the lewd story about Filenio Sisterno (night 2, story 2) became part of England's narrative stock in William Painter's enormously popular *Palace of Pleasure* (1566–67 et seq.), while "The Tailor's Apprentice" (night 8, story 4) was produced as a chapbook.

Erotic titillation and a taste for bathroom humor fueled a market for a third wave of printings in France, Germany, and England between 1890 and 1910. The foolishly archaicized Richard Burton translation published in English by the notorious Carrington in Paris (1906) is based on but is far inferior to W. G. Waters's careful and generally accurate translation of 1894.

A fourth wave of publication, this one scholarly, began in 1898 with Giuseppe Rua's Italian edition of the *Pleasant Nights*, which initiated an interest in Straparola's tales among modern scholars. Rua's edition was followed by Giovanni Machia's 1943 edition, Manlio Pastore Stocchi's edition of 1975, and Donato Pirovano's in 2000. In France Louveau and Larivey's translation was revised by Joël Gayraud and published in 1999 in conjunction with the Centre Nationale du Livre in the series Collection Merveilleux.

The Lasting Legacy of Straparola's Stories: Puss in Boots

Of all Straparola's stories, the tale of Costantino and his cat most perfectly and completely embodied the dream of a social rise through magic and marriage (see Chapter 1). It has also exerted the most lasting influence of any of Straparola's rise tales.

After Straparola's death his Costantino story went in two different directions, the first of which took it south. Peddlers' packs and asses' backs provided one southward route, and Venetian bookmen sold abundantly to the Kingdom of Naples, as Paul Grendler pointed out (1977, 16). On the other hand, uncounted thousands of known performances of various "Puss in Boots" plays in the nineteenth and twentieth centuries attest to the theatrical suitability of the story's plot and characterizations. Hence Straparola's story may equally well have made its way to Naples on streetplayers' feet, where it would eventually become "Cagliuso," the fourth tale on the second day of Giambattista Basile's *Cunto de li cunti* (1634), now known as the *Pentamerone*.

Students of living theater well know that the location where and audience before whom a play is performed condition the words spoken on the stage, and so it should come as no surprise that, by the time Basile composed his version of Straparola's story, his cat brought not a rabbit but one of Naples's ubiquitous fish to the king. And consistent with a general weakening of women and their roles in tale collections that was slowly but incrementally taking place in Europe (Bottigheimer 2000), Basile transformed Straparola's cat/mother Soriana into an impoverished *father*. His hero, renamed Cagliuso, was one of only two brothers rather than Straparola's three, but he still remained as weakly ineffectual as Costantino had been. Basile's Cagliuso was also more flawed in personal terms: he'd vowed to respectfully embalm the cat after her death and reverentially display her body in a golden cage, yet, when the cat pretended to have died, Cagliuso, basely ungrateful, roughly declared that somebody ought to "take [her] by the paws and throw [her] out the window" (trans. Penzer; see also Canepa 1999, chap. 6).[5]

The principal difference between Basile's version of Straparola's cat story was one that reflected social class, and it developed naturally from the major shift in the kind of audience he addressed. Basile originally presented his story and its hero not for apprentices, artisans, and their wives and sisters, but for members of his literary society in Naples, the

Oziosi. Highly literate, courtly, and well-versed in baroque rhetoric, such listeners must have tacitly encouraged Basile to scrub away the gritty bits of Venetian poverty from his hero. Scabrousness remained, but Basile transferred it from the hero to the repulsively sniveling company of female storytellers he created to tell the tale, so that it was they, and not the hero, who bore the filthy signs of urban indigence. Basile's elevated audience was not a hungry one, either, and consequently he omitted the hero's hunger, a miserable state so often present in Straparola's stories. He also left out the dexterous fairy cat's sweeping "all sorts of good provender, when no one was looking that way" (trans. Penzer) from the king's table into a bag that she took home to her master. These were details with which Basile's audience would not have identified. If a Neapolitan street version of the tale had included the hero's hunger, Basile edited that part of the story out of his retelling.

By far the more influential branch of Costantino's story traveled north. Translated into French by Pierre de Larivey (1540–1612), it had been published in *Facétieuses nuictes* in Lyons and Paris by the 1570s. De Larivey maintained Straparola's plot and its details almost entirely intact, giving French endings to the characters' names. Straparola's Costantino Fortunato became de Larivey's Constantin le Fortuné, the youngest of three sons of a poverty-stricken "Soriane." De Larivey retained the cat's female gender, respectfully calling her "Madame la Chatte," but he had Constantin plunge into the cleansing river a formulaic three times and had the cat lick him from his foot all the way to his head to clear away his scurvy and his mange (*teigne, gale*).

From de Larivey's "Costantin Fortuné" to Charles Perrault's "Master Cat" there were very few steps. Paragraph for paragraph, Perrault's story matched de Larivey's, which must have lain open on the writing desk before him as he composed his courtly version of Straparola's original story. All the more telling, then, are the changes that Perrault made to de Larivey's text.[6]

Times were changing. The general process by which female characters in European fairy tales were weakened and disempowered was continuing (Bottigheimer 2000), and fathers were increasingly superseding mothers in narrative importance. Thus it is not surprising that Perrault replaced his hero's expiring mother with a dying father, a poor miller. In yet another narrative masculinization, de Larivey's female "Madame Chatte" became Perrault's male "Le Maistre Chat." Perrault also dropped "Dussolin," "Tésifon," and "Constantin le Fortuné," the three un-French names de Larivey had carefully preserved from Straparola's text, and instead had his "Master Cat" provide the hero with the faked noble title, the "marquis de Carabas."

Perrault deepened the chasm separating the youngest from the two elder brothers by changing Straparola's mother's bequests—a bread trough, a pasta board, and a cat—to a father's two inheritances that could be turned to good financial account—a mill and a donkey for the older boys—leaving only an unpromising cat for the youngest.

Like the heroes and heroines of stories intended for bourgeois or noble readers (Bottigheimer 1990), Perrault made his hero perform a slightly more active role in effectuating his own social rise. At Master Cat's request, the "marquis" provided the now-famous boots to protect puss's paws from woodland roughness.

Perrault kept the rabbit that both Straparola's and de Larivey's cats had delivered to the king, but raised it to the level of *haute cuisine* as a "Lapin de Garenne," the culinary equivalent of the "Sauce Robert" he had introduced into "Sleeping Beauty." Consistent with his readers' refined experience, Perrault added game (*gibier*) and partridges (*perdrix*) to Master Cat's gifts to the king. And true to the refined sensibilities of his circle of friends, he brought elevated emotion into the fairy tale marriage by having the king's daughter fall madly in love (*elle en devint amoureuse à la folie*) with the sham "marquis."

What Perrault removed from de Larivey's translation is just as telling, for it indicates the extent to which Perrault addressed the putative expectations of his intended audience. First of all, he deleted the cat's supplying his hungry master with food pilfered from the king's table, and he omitted the cat's cleansing of the hero's mangy skin. In other words, Perrault erased Straparola's and de Larivey's realistic descriptions of the hunger and disease so prevalent among the poor of sixteenth-century Venice and Paris as well as among impoverished inhabitants of famine-ridden seventeenth-century France.

Perrault's version of "Puss in Boots" remained a *rise* tale, but one that addressed a propertied readership with corresponding experience and expectations. In Perrault's rise tale, the falsified appearance of riches preceded marriage, as his princess's father "verified" the hero's possession of great wealth before the nuptials took place. His royal behavior was consistent with seventeenth-century concerns surrounding the important event of entering into an alliance by marriage and overrode Straparola's and de Larivey's paradigm.

Perrault had been away from the Versailles court of Louis XIV for well over a decade when he composed his collection of fairy tales. In Paris he lived several streets away from the high-minded nuns of Port-Royal and had enough mutual friends with them to be considered part of their outer circle. He was himself a man who had rejected an advantageous match proposed by his mentor, the powerful minister Jean-Baptiste Colbert, in order to marry a woman he loved. When his wife died young, he undertook his children's education himself. It is therefore not surprising that a man who married for love did not allow base emotions to drive heroes' and heroines' actions as they so often did in Straparola's and Basile's tales, especially their "Puss in Boots" stories. Straparola's heroes were often vengeful, and his Costantino was certainly unmannerly when he refused to share his "good provender" with his brothers. Like Straparola, Basile had also flawed his hero with ingratitude. Perrault, on the other hand, took elaborate precautions in order to keep his "marquis" perfectly virtuous: he crafted conversations that allowed his hero to encourage the king to believe that he owned the vast estates through which their entourage was passing, but carefully refrained from a single instance of overt lying:

"You have a fine patrimony there," said the king to the marquis of Carabas. "You see, Sire," responded the marquis, "it's a meadow that never fails to produce well every single year."

(Vous avez là un bel heritage, dit le Roy au Marquis de Carabas. Vous voyez, Sire, répondit le Marquis, c'est un pré qui ne manque point de rapporter abondament toutes les années.)

In this passage Perrault allowed his hero to speak substantial truth in order to convey an essential untruth. The practice worked well as a marriage strategy, for the final result was that the king, impressed with the marquis of Carabas's holdings, allowed him to marry his daughter.

Other Stories

In addition to Costantino's cat, other Straparola stories also lived on in the works of later authors. Mme de Murat readily admitted in the "Avertissement" of *Histoires sublimes et allégoriques* (1699) that fairytale authors of her generation, including herself, turned to Straparola's collection for plots and characters. Mme de Murat's assertion is easily corroborated within her own oeuvre, since she reformulated Straparola's "Prince Pig" into her "Roy porc" and his "Pietro Pazzo" into her "Turbot."

Mme d'Aulnoy and her literary acquaintances, all titled or wealthy or both, read to one another in dazzling painted and tapestried salons. The glittering audience before whom they performed differed fundamentally from the humble ones that form part of the readership for whom Straparola had composed his rise tales. In most cases, Mme d'Aulnoy adopted the French names of Straparola's characters given them by de Larivey. But in other respects she reworked Straparola's tales within the conventions of seventeenth-century French preciosity by decorating them with gem-studded and flower-bedecked images and by extending them with subplots whose fairyland antagonists threw obstacles in the path traveled by her heroes and heroines as they sought true love and lasting union with their beloveds.

Mme d'Aulnoy's "Le prince marcassin" and Count Hamilton's "Pertharite and Ferrandine" are related to "Prince Pig" (night 2, story 1), just as Mme d'Aulnoy's "Le Dauphin" recreates "Peter the Fool" (night 3, story 1). Straparola's "Biancabella" (night 3, story 3), his "Fortunio" (night 3, story 4), his "Ancilotto" (night 4, story 3), and his "Guerrino" (night 5, story 1) underlie Mme d'Aulnoy's "Blanchebelle," her "Oiseau bleu," her "Belle Étoile," and her "Prince Guerin," in that order. Mme d'Aulnoy reworked only Straparola's restoration and rise tales (though not his Costantino "Puss in Boots" tale, which evidently didn't appeal to her), leaving aside all other genres represented in his collection. It is remarkable, if not amazing, that Marc Soriano, in writing for the reference book of record, the *Enzyklopädie des Märchens*, acknowledged none of Mme d'Aulnoy's indebtedness to Straparola, imputing their content instead solely to oral sources.

Through the lengthy literary fairy tales of Mme d'Aulnoy and her literary acquaintances, Straparolean magical motifs entered the arena of late seventeenth- and early eighteenth-century French *contes de fées*. The French literary effloresence that followed spread Straparola's stories along with their magical motifs into France, England, and Germany. From the genre they established, two major literary forms emerged: the literary fairy tale that continued the tradition Mme d'Aulnoy developed and exemplified; and the "folk" style that carried on Perrault's model.[7]

The study of motifs and their distribution patterns in the age of print differs fundamentally from assertions about narrative ancestry based on a single motif referred to in "oral tradition." Motifs in the age of print exist within a thick layer of evidence that includes publishing histories, literacy rates, distribution patterns, and surviving texts, all of which taken together enable researchers to query motif transmission and reappearance. One of the more perplexing similarities between one of Straparola's stories and a narrative descendent is the uncannily close relationship between "Ancilotto" (night 4, story 3) and Antoine Galland's tale of Princess Parizade and her envious sisters. Galland included it with tales he reputedly translated from an unspecified Eastern source, which led W. G. Waters to conclude either that Galland had looked at and then had adopted Straparola's fable, or that Straparola had gotten it from an Eastern source himself (1898, 4: 248). In 1765 Carlo Gozzi made "Ancilotto" into a theatrical fairy tale, "L'Augellin belverde." In Italy "Ancilotto" had so penetrated the awareness of the reading and listening public that it was still circulating in the nineteenth century. In V. Imbriani's collection it was No. 6, "L'uccellino che parla"; Giuseppe Pitré collected it at the other end of Italy in Sicily in 1875. The same was true of Straparola's "Prince Pig" (night 2, story 1), which Imbriani found in Florence in 1877 (No. 17) and Laura Gonzenbach recorded in Sicily a few years later.

In Germany, Clemens Brentano owned three copies of *Piacevoli notti*, one each in Italian, French, and German, and they obviously came into play when he composed *Urchronika*. Long thought to be based on Hero and Leander, its details match Straparola's tale of "Malgherita Spolatina and the Hermit" (night 7, story 2) far more closely than they do that of the classical Hero and Leander (Hosch 1986, 216–33).

In the Grimms' collection, too, numerous tales resuscitate Straparolean stories discussed in this study. "Prince Pig" (night 3, story 1) became No. 108, "Hans mein Igel"; "Livoretto" (night 3, story 2) turned into No. 17, "Die weisse Schlange"; "Ancilotto" (night 4, story 3) returned as No. 96, "De drei Vügelkens"; "Guerrino" (night 5, story 1) underlay No. 136, "Der Eisenhans"; "The Three Brothers" (night 7, story 5) was the same as No. 129, "Die vier Brüder"; "The Tailor's Apprentice" (night 8, story 4) told the same story as No. 68, "De Gaudeif un sien Meester."

Straparola's "Magic Doll" had direct descendants in Italy, Spain, and Germany. Ludwig Bechstein took it into his *Neues Deutsches Märchenbuch* (1856 et seq.) as No. 50, "Dukaten-Angele," where the doll produced golden "Gackele" for her adoring owner but stinking "eggs" for anyone else. The standard rise tale formula of rags-magic-marriage-riches, however, was altered when Bechstein had the sisters grow rich from the doll's gold alone, for he omitted the doll's clawing grip on the king's behind and his consequent desperate search for relief from his misery.

A Heritage of Motifs and Episodes

The transmission of entire stories were not the only way Straparola's legacy can be measured. Motifs also played a part. The restoration tale heroine Biancabella (night 3, story 3) was born with a collar of intricately worked gold around her neck. She incorporated jewelry into her body just as did the nameless daughter in the Grimms' "Twelve Swans" (No. 9) who bore a golden star on her forehead. Biancabella also produced a stock of pearls and precious stones whenever she combed her hair. In so doing, she set a style for countless fairytale good sisters' wealth-producing bodies, whether it was in Charles Perrault's "Les Fées," in "Les Enchantements de l'éloquence" by his niece Mlle Marie Jeanne L'Héritier, in Giambattista Basile's "Le Doie pizzele," or in the Grimms' "Frau Holle" (No. 24).

In some cases episodes that have long puzzled fairytale scholars can be found in Straparola's tales. One such puzzle occurs in the Grimms' "Frog Prince" (No. 1), when the king's daughter throws the frog with all her strength against the wall. Over the years of his editing Grimm added an adverb, "furiously" (*bitterböse*) to supply a credible emotional motivation for the princess's violent act, but in the first edition, she simply *did* it. Her act echoed the bedroom episode in Straparola's "The Tailor's Apprentice" (night 8, story 4), where Dionigi instructed his beloved Princess Violante to save him from the anger of his former employer, Lattanzio, by throwing the ruby, into which he would have turned himself, against the wall, fiercely and with all her strength. That, he told her, would change the ruby into a fine large pomegranate that would break open and scatter its ruby-colored seeds over the floor (see Chapter 1 for the rest of the story). Straparola's motif lived on in the Grimms' "Frog-King" (KHM 1) in strange isolation from its original narrative context, when the princess inexplicably hurled the frog against the wall of her chamber.

Straparola's plots were flexible because their bare bones provided narrative skeletons that later authors could flesh out according to the audience they addressed. Basile could make Peter the Fool into a figure of fun for Neapolitan intellectuals and Mme d'Aulnoy could fashion from him a romantic figure that suited her friends on the Ile St. Louis. Straparola's Costantino Fortunato spoke to the longings of a reading public with a taste for stories that would compensate for a dreary daily existence.

Straparola introduced magic into brief tales that promised wealth. In doing that, he relayed restoration tales and invented rise tales for a Venetian public that was hungry for the promise of wealth. Similar reading publics existed in Italy, France, Germany, and Spain, and they would continue to savor his stories as he had written them and as they had been rewritten by others for another 250 years.

For Straparola's readers, fiction was a sieve that held back the hard unyielding facts of daily lives and let dreams and longings pass through. An imagined marriage rather than daily toil must have seemed an ideal route to remote riches. Straparola's fairy tales of rags-to-riches through magic and marriage—urban creations for an urban readership with an urban worldview—lent their readers and listeners enduring hope for magically-mediated future wealth.

Notes

Chapter 1

1. Erhard Lommatzsch's *Beiträge zur älteren italienischen Volksdichtung* (1950, 1963) made available texts of the Wolfenbüttel collection of early popular imprints, which include a large number of secular romances intended for performance.

2. From this perspective one might apply Propp's "lack" and "lack liquidated." What is important is not the simple acquisition of wealth, but the means and timing of obtaining it.

3. Literally, the right to "join her" (*copularla*) in marriage, which could be punningly delivered as a broadly expressed sexual act.

4. Amazed, because she knew them to live a "buona vita e sí oneste del corpo loro che opposizione alcuna non pativano." In other words, they were not prostituting themselves to earn the goods evident in their house.

5. Violante connotes not "violent" but the title of a portrait by Titian of a stunningly beautiful Venetian courtesan whose name derived from the violet she was wearing.

Chapter 2

1. Necromancy was defined as a form of high magic that required the study of esoteric textbooks. It differed from the simple nonacademic act of "conjuration"or "divination," which used the "sympathetic" magic of charms and incantations, folk medical "healings," the maleficent magic of "maleficium," and satanism, the last of which did not form a significant part of the practice of magic in Renaissance Venice. Magic in Venice, which had lost touch with agrarian practices, was distinctly urban in its form and aims. Five hundred cases of the practice of magic were brought before the Venetian Inquisition between 1542 and 1650. See Martin (1989, 5–8).

2. "The Tailor's Apprentice" migrated to England, where it was published in William Painter's sixteenth-century *Palace of Pleasure*. It lived on in subsequent reprints and also as a freestanding chapbook, *The Italian Taylor and His Boy* (London: T.P., 1609 et seq.).

Chapter 3

1. See Chapter 4, n. 17 for the full text of the privilege.

2. My thanks to Professor Martin Lowry at the University of Warwick for commenting on and clarifying the specific meaning of this phrase in the context of sixteenth-century Venetian publishing.

3. "In hoc enim oppido inclytae stirpis sfortiadum antiquo feudo ortum habuit Io. Franciscus Straparola cujus liber saepe editus circumfertur italice hoc programmate: 'Le tredici piacevolissimi notti overo favole ed enimmi'" (Arisius 1741, cited in Straparola 1898, 4:269).

4. The first extant historical account was composed by a seventeenth-century cleric, Donato Calvi, *Delle grandezze della Madonna SS di Caravaggio* (Milan: d'Agnelli, 1710).

5. One scholar, A. Mazzi (1909), suggested that Straparola's natal family was well off, based on an *ex libris* in a book housed in the Bergamo Municipal Library that names a "Io Franc Streparolle." Spelling of proper names was flexible, and the given names, Giovan Francesco (Latin Io. Franc.) were common in the late 1400s and early 1500s. Ann Motte (1972, 167) also believed that his natal family was in comfortable circumstances, identifying them as the Secco, who had first been proposed as his family of origin in the early 1700s (Rua 1890a, 15:113n1). Her assumption may rest on the speculation cited by Demnati from Lancetti's *Bibliografia Cremonense*, namely, that Straparola might have come from the "famille Secchi de Caravage, qui était une famille aisée" (Demnati 1989, 181n56). However, no basis exists for assuming that Straparola stemmed from one of Caravaggio's noble families, and the language of the sonnet in which he refers to a member of the Secco family (see below) suggests social distance from them.

6. Fermo, a citizen of Bergamo and the scion of a noble family, distributed his wealth to the poor. Rustico and Fermo were kinsmen. They are said to have revived a dead man after leaving Caravaggio by the Porta Vicinato. Martyrs, both were beheaded outside Verona in the third century.

7. Saint Bernardino of Siena (1380–1444) had brought peace between Caravaggio and Treviglio in 1421 by preaching from a mobile pulpit carried to the boundary between the two territories (Scaperotta 2000, sheet 6).

8. The seventeenth-century historian Calvi claimed a population of 13,000 in the late sixteenth and early seventeenth centuries (cited in Secco d'Aragona 1968, 17). This seems an unrealistically high estimate, given the physical limitations of the town's size.

9. Zambò's story already existed, with a "Zanni" as hero, but earlier Zanni stories offered only an itinerary from Brescia to Venice, without the Venetian details Straparola supplied. See also below for a story by Antonio Molino about another Bergamo emigrant. According to Brian Pullan, Bandello portrayed a real person, Gioan Antonio Dolce, as "Fracasso of Bergamo," a Bergamo emigrant who made his way to Genoa (Pullan 1999, 216).

10. The fact that the author of *Pleasant Nights* appears to have warmly identified himself with a knowledge of Latin in his version of the stories of Cesare Napolitano (night 13, story 10) and Maestro Gotfreddo (night 13, story

12) does not prove that Straparola knew Latin well, since the stories of night 13 came from Morlini's collection and may have been the work of a different authorial hand (see Chapter 4).

11. "Sonnet cxiiii O Charavagio," O Charavagio castel venturato / come felice ti trovi al presente / godendo miser Iacomo pesente / che ti ten per virtu tanto inalciato. // Come per honorare e al mondo nato / come la gloria sua volar si sente / secunda in ogni banda ancor ch'absente/ si trovi col saper: da ognun desiato. // Regna in colui dogni virtude de el fiore / seco a le muse: secoelises monte / qual e dogni saper splendido honore // Ardito e nel parlar humel in fronte / nel rider dolce in pecto pien damore / dogni scientia al fin un archa & fonte." The text is taken from the 1515 edition, whose spelling differs slightly from the 1508 edition.

12. In other sonnets he used the second person singular in addressing a person; see below.

13. Giuseppe Rua understood Iacomo as someone with the surname Pesente, which I view as a misreading. See Rua (1890a, 112).

14. Rua cites accounts published in 1580 and 1590 detailing similar journeys of a "Zani" (Johnny) from Brescia to Venice, but they lack the details of Straparola's account. The name they all give to their heros is a north Italian form of John (Zoan or Zuan) made more colloquial as "Zambo," as a process of assimilation to the following labial *b* changes the *n* to *m*. American readers will recognize the analogy with affectionate forms of male names such as "Jimbo" or "Timbo."

15. Hanging in the Gallerie dell'Accademie in Venice, the painting is reproduced in Brown (1997, 99, fig. 67).

16. Note that Straparola here carelessly omits the fact that the mainland community of Fusina can't be reached by walking.

17. For more on public violence, see Davis (1994).

18. Indirect evidence about literacy rates in Italy points toward high rates of urban literacy. In late 1500s Venice there were 250 schoolteachers in a population of 135,000, which translates to one for every 135 males under the age of 20, for which documentation Peter Burke cites Cipolla (1969) and Baldo (1977) (Burke 1987, 111). He concluded cautiously that "literacy in northern Italy … was high relative to other parts of Europe" except for the Netherlands between 1000 and 1600 (1987, 112).

19. Burke draws on Mortier (1930) and Logan (1972) for this information.

20. Burke makes the point that Bandello dedicated each of his stories to a different noble person and contrasts his practice with the "Venetian 'Grub Street', just off the Grand Canal" (118). In this regard, it is worth noting that Bandello had originally performed his tales at the court of Mantua in the 1520s, had not published them in print, and only committed them to print in the 1550s. At the time he did not live in or near Venice, but was a bishop in a remote area of France. See also Chapter 4.

21. The latter name was undoubtedly meant as a pun on Florence's famous Accademia Liviana Pordenon, renamed the Perseraventi in 1515, which counted Michelangelo among its members.

22. These districts regularly had greater interests on the mainland than the districts of S. Croce and S. Polo (Gullino 1994 passim).

23. I conclude this from the fact that the printer he approached, Comin da Trino, rarely took full financial responsibility for the books he printed (Richardson 1999, 35), so that Straparola would have had to ante up at the very least the cost of the paper for the first edition.

24. The fingerprints of the first and second printings are different. For a discussion of fingerprints, see Vriesema (1986) and Dijstelberge (1997).

25. "State felici, memore di quelli, che nel core scolpite vi tengono, tra quali non credo esser il minimo." From *Piacevoli Notti* (Venice: Comin da Trino, 1553) (A ii^v).

26. Paul Grendler kindly pointed out that one contemporary artist, Enea Vico da Parma, did a series of portraits for the Venetian publisher Francesco Marcolini that provided generic author portraits. If the portrait in question is one of those, I have not encountered it in mid-sixteenth-century facing pages.

27. For a systematic history and description of frontispiece portraits, see "Ritratto" in Barberi (1969, 1: 117–20) and illustrative plates 2: 17, 71, 72, 107, 112, 119, 124, 130. My assumption that the lack of a frame for Straparola's authorial portrait is significant is based on my own observations of authorial or subject portraits in scores of sixteenth- and seventeenth-century books.

28. The date given is "XI Gennaio 1554," which, given the fact that Venice's year began on March 1 in those years, translates as 11 January 1555.

29. "State felici, memori di me" (A iii^v).

30. Pirovano, who scoured Venetian necrologies through the 1550s and into the 1560s without finding his name (2000, liv), holds that Straparola died before the 1557 edition appeared, based on the existence of errors in the text. See Pirovano (2000, 2: 817–18). However, since all the editions are flawed, errors in the 1557 edition aren't significant in my view.

Chapter 4

1. For page counts the Rua edition works well because there are no footnotes to alter the number of pages required by the text of a story. In any case, it is the relative not the actual length that is significant.

2. A few of the texts that have been listed as sources share only a single motif with the story in question. That is hardly sufficient to establish a real-world connection. In other cases, as in the stories taken over wholesale from Morlini on the eleventh, twelfth, and thirteenth nights, an unmistakably clear relationship exists.

3. A mixed readership had been visible on the "cover" of the first edition of Straparola's *Opera nova* (1508), on which the printer had pictured both men and women as potential readers, but these readers were upper class, not artisanal.

4. It is consistent with the likelihood that someone else finished Book 2 that it was not a classical story or a story element that was casually inserted

toward the end of the collection (night 12, story 3), but a mention of Aristotle's *Politics*!

5. There has to be a palpable reason why only the second printing of Book 1 was sold at the sign of the Diamond near Saint Luke. Although he ultimately decided to place it with the much better located Libraria della Colombina behind the Fondaco dei Tedeschi, for personal reasons he may have decided that he should sell at least one of the printings at the Diamond.

6. The fact that Straparola constructed his frametale with ten female storytellers suggests that his original intention was to produce a ten-night sequence, a literary allusion to the *Decameron*'s ten-*day* story sequence.

7. Any bookseller in mid-century Venice would have been well aware of the fact that Venetian printers such as Lucantonio Giunta, Nicolini da Sabbio, Alouise de Tortis, and Girolamo Scotto had produced editions of *Orlando inamorato* in the 1530s and 1540s and that other printers such as Giovanni Andrea Valvasore and Gabriel Girolito de Ferrari has produced editions of *Orlando Furioso* in the same period. See also Richardson 1999 59.

8. In addition to Boiardo's *Orlando inammorato* and Ariosto's *Orlando furioso*, a bestseller of the 1500s, many other romances had come on the market. They included Francesco de'Lodovici, *L'Antheo gigante* in the 1520s; Nicolò Liburnio, *Selvette* (short works in prose and verse); Christoforo, called "L'Altissimo," *Historia de Anthenore*, ca. 1519; Bernardo Giambullari, *Ciriffo Calvaneo*, ca 1514; Andrea da Barberino, *Gerrin Meschino*. See Richardson (1999, 73, 75, 91, 116).

9. A ducat consisted of 3.5 grams of gold. This amount is based on prices available for a book of light songs, entertaining literature similar to the *Pleasant Nights* (Richardson 1999, 61). The paper in surviving copies of Straparola's books is of a good to middling grade, and could well have cost more than 70–75 ducats for a print run of 1000 copies.

10. These are all booksellers through whom Comin da Trino distributed books he had printed. There were several other booksellers who commissioned him to print books for themselves. See Donvito 1997 310. Straparola's book was not placed with any of these booksellers, but was to be had instead "at the sign of S. Alvise." It is perhaps an insider's joke that, instead of Comin da Trino, the title page of the 1551 printing *Pleasant Nights* listed Orpheo dalla Carta as printer (Appresso Orpheo dalla Carta), who appeared again in the book's dedicatory letter, praising Straparola to potential readers. Unlike Donato Pirovano I believe that Orfeo dalla Carta was Straparola's imaginary creation.

11. Vincenza Donvito reports that Comin da Trino was called before the Holy Office on 22 August 1547 and that sometime during 1548 he was interrogated about an unspecified, but perhaps Calvinist, *Catechismo* he had printed. On 10 November 1548 Comin da Trino had received an "instruction" about another book, Calmo's *I piacevoli Discorsi*. Furthermore, on 23 May 1549 another book of his, a discourse on penitence, was recalled at the instance of the Holy Office. Comin himself was involved with a Reformed group that practiced reading aloud from Scripture. See Donvito (1997, 308–9).

12. In considering the *Pleasant Nights*, Suzanne Magnanini sites the pig's monstrosity within a sixteenth-century discourse on monstrous births. See Magnanini (2000).

13. This murder was retold in *Lamento del Duca Galeazo Maria, Duca di Milano*, but Ottaviano Maria is not mentioned in the lament's 153 lines. A Florentine edition of 1568 is reprinted in Lommatzsch (1950, 4: 236–41).

14. Giuseppe Rua notes yet other discrepancies between Straparola's and contemporaneous historical versions of events surrounding Ottaviano Maria Sforza's life (Rua 1890, 15: 133 ff.).

15. It is notable that Straparola favored Sforza names over those of the Caravaggio Secco family in all its branches. During Straparola's lifetime they bore names such as Antonio, (Gian) Fermo, (Gian) Francesco, (Gian) Bernardino, Marco, Gian Luigi, Giuseppe, Nicolò, Orazio, Lancellotto, Carlo, Giorgio, Isaia, Barnabas. Socino, Marcantonio (Secco 1968, 295–302).

16. Straparola wrote (night 2, introduction): "Di che le donne e parimente gli uomini fecero sí gran risa, che ancora ridono." Boccaccio had written (night 3, story 10): "di che esse fecero sí gran risa, che ancor ridono" (Pirovano 2000, 94n1).

17. For more on Burchiella, see Magnanini (2000, 45n66).

18. A similar distancing would have been understood from the fact that Comin da Trino had printed *Pleasant Nights* "ad instanza dall'autore," as the colophon of Book 2 (1553) indicates.

19. For very brief comments on Straparola's narrators, see Barsch (1988, 157–61).

20. Ambrogio de Predis's portrait of Queen Bianca Maria Sforza was painted in 1495 and thus predates this period. Titian's portrait of the countess Isabella d'Este was done in 1534/5, very nearly at the time set for the fictive storytelling gathering. Both portraits hang in the Kunsthistorisches Museum in Vienna. Tintoretto's portrait of the Soranzo family hangs in the Sforza Castle in Milan.

21. These portraits also hang in the Kunsthistorisches Museum in Vienna.

22. Straparola put the coarsely obscene story of three nuns' urinary, rectal, and buttock skills (night 6, story 4) into Antonio Bembo's mouth.

23. Register of the Archivio di Stato di Venezia, Senato Terra, filza 37, carta 4ᵛ, as cited by Pirovano (2000, "Nota Biografica," 1: liii): "Che per autorità di questo Conseglio sia concesso al R.do Padre Don Calisto da Piacenza, canonico regolare, et Predicatore Apostolico, che alcuno altro, che lui senza sua permissione possa stampare, né far stampare, né vendere in alcun loco del Do[minio] nostro, etiam che fossero stampate altrove le enarratione delli Evangelij da lui composte per anni x prossimi, sotto pena di perdere l'opere, et de ducati cento alli contrafacenti ogni fiata, che contrafarano; la qual pena sia divisa per terzo fra l'accusatore, il magistrato che farà l'essecutione et l'Arsenà nostro. —Et il medesimo sia concesso a Zuan Francesco Sstraparola da Caravaggio per l'opera volgare da lui composta, titolata le piacevoli notti; essendo obligati tutti loro d'osservare quello, che per le nostre leggi è disposto in materia di stampe—."

The privilege was signed by Ludovico Barbadico, Tommaso Contareno (Contarini), Francesco Veniero (Venier), and Zaccaria Duodo.

24. Another weighty reason for assuming that Straparola had only presented the stories of Book 1 in his privilege application lies in the fact that the third story of the ninth night appears to derive from a book published in "January 1550" (1551 by the modern calendar). See Rua (1890a, 128).

25. Pirovano (2000) has hypothesized that Orfeo dalla Carta was a coded name for a member of a Venetian stationer's family who was Straparola's financial backer for the publication of his stories. For additional comment see note 9.

26. Cottino-Jones (2000, 175) understands Straparola's anachronistic blossoming and leafing out as an expression of the "fantastic" rather than as one of many compositional errors, as I do.

27. It is interesting, and possibly relevant for Straparola's personal world of belief, that the *canzone* patterning in Book 1 bears a resemblance to the abracadabra amulet (Burke 1987, 122): a / ab / abr / abra / abrac / abraca / abracad / abracada / abracadab / abracadabr / abracadabra.

28. For the increasing involvement of editors in Venetian publishing in the sixteenth century, see Richardson (1994, 2, 103). Their work was often directed at norming usage and spelling in accordance with fourteenth-century Tuscan usage (64–89).

29. The literature on copyright, plagiarism, and literary theft has grown enormously in recent years, with the largest component, however, devoted to English and French practice. For sixteenth-century Italy see Padoan (1985).

Chapter 5

1. British Library 12470.f.3.

2. This edition is known only from its privilege, dated 1569. See Senn (1993, 49).

3. The close succession of printings theoretically leaves open the opposite possibility that the tales did *not* sell, namely, that each apparently new printing may have represented simply a repackaging of unsold sheets. Checking the fingerprints of these volumes, however, will readily clarify this point.

4. It would be interesting to compare the fingerprints of the 1791 and 1817 printings to see if the 1817 text consisted of unsold 1791 sheets shipped to Berlin and provided with a new title page.

5. Penzer translated the cat's gender as masculine; Canepa's translation returns its original femaleness.

6. Denise Escarpit's thorough study of the publishing history of "Le chat botté" / "Puss in Boots" in French and English takes Perrault's text as its beginning point. With respect to the tale's origins, she noted only that "les *Piacevoli Notti* et *Lo Cunto de li Cunti* sont des sources très probables de Perrault" (52).

7. This is worked out in detail in Bottigheimer (2002).

Bibliography

Anonymous. 1582. *Passa-Tempo de' Curiosi, Nel quale si trovano compendiati, sali-leggiadri, motti acuti, facezie piacevoli, butte ridiculose e bisticci finissimi; Operetta in cui l'utile contrasta co'l curioso, l'acuto co'l facile e'l vago co'l breve. Tolta e raccolta da varii e più sensati Autori, da Giovanni Mülmann/ Lipsia MDCLXXXII. Con licenza de' Superiori lo stampò Cristiano Götze.* Leipzig: Christian Götze. Copy in British Library.

Anonymous. 1991. *Profili storici ed economici: Caravaggio.* Monza: Editrice Universale.

Apo, Satu. 1988. "The Two Worlds of the Finnish Fairytale: Observations on the Folk and Literary Fairytale Tradition of the 19th Century." *ARV: Journal of Scandinavian Folklore* 44: 27–48.

Apuleius, Lucius. 1549. *L. Apvlegio tradotto in volgare.* Trans. M. M. Bojardo. Venice: Bartolomeo l'Imperatore and Francesco Veneziano.

Arisius, Franciscus. 1741. *Cremona illustrata.* Cremona: Petrum Ricchini.

Aulnoy, Mme Marie-Catherine de Barneville, Comtesse d'. 1997. *Les Contes des fées.* Intro. Jacques Barchilon, ed. Philippe Hourcade. Paris: Société des Textes Français Modernes.

Baader, Renate. 1986. *Dames de lettres: Autorinnen des preziösen, hocharistokratis-chen und "modernen" Salons (1649–1698): Mlle de Scudéry—Mlle de Monpen-sier—Mme d'Aulnoy.* Stuttgart: Metzler.

Barberi, Francesco. 1969. *Il Frontespizio nel libro italiano del quattrocento e del cinquecento.* 2 vols. Documenti sulle Arti del Libro 7. Milan: Edizioni il Polifilo.

Barsch, Karl Heinrich. 1988. "The 'Eternal Womanly' in Novella Narration: Female Roles in the Frames of Boccaccio's Decameron, Straparola's Piacevoli Notti, the Queen of Navarre's Heptameron, and Goethe's Unter-haltungen deutscher Ausgewanderten." In *Studies in Modern and Classical Languages and Literatures,* ed. Fidel López-Criado. Madrid: Origenes. 155–62.

Bechstein, Ludwig. 1856/1965. *Sämtliche Märchen.* Munich: Winkler Verlag.

Boccaccio, Giovanni. 1353/1982. *Decameron.* Berkeley: University of California Press.

Bonomo, G. 1958. "Motivi magico-stregonici in una novella dello Straparola." *Rassegna della Letterature Italiana* 62: 365–69.

Bottigheimer, Ruth B. 1987. *Grimms' Bad Girls and Bold Boys: The Moral and Social Vision of the Tales.* New Haven, Conn.: Yale University Press.

———. 1989. "Fairy Tales, Folk Narrative Research, and History." *Social History* 14,1: 343–57.

———. 1990. "Ludwig Bechstein's Fairy Tales: Nineteenth-Century Bestsellers and Bürgerlichkeit." *Internationales Archiv für Sozialgeschichte der deutschen Literatur* 15, 2: 655–88.

———. 1993. "Luckless, Witless, and Filthy-Footed: A Socio-Cultural Study and Publishing History Analysis of 'The Lazy Boy' (AT 675)." *Journal of American Folklore* 106, 421: 259–84.

———. 1994. "Straparola's *Piacevoli Notti*: Rags-to-Riches Fairy Tales as Urban Creations." *Marvels and Tales* 8, 2: 281–96.

———. 1998. Review of Lewis C. Seifert, *Fairy Tales, Sexuality and Gender in France 1690–1715* (Cambridge: Cambridge University Press, 1997). *Fabula* 39, 1/2 (1998): 160–62.

———. 2000. "Fertility Control and the Birth of the Modern European Fairy Tale Heroine." *Marvels and Tales* 14, 1: 64–79.

———. 2002. "Elevated Inceptions and Popular Outcomes: The Contes of Marie-Catherine d'Aulnoy and Charles Perrault." *elo*, forthcoming.

Brakelmann, F. W. J. 1867. *Giovan Francesco Straparola da Caravaggio*. Göttingen: E. A. Huth.

Brown, Patricia Fortini. 1997. *Art and Life in Renaissance Venice*. New York: Abrams.

Burke, Peter. 1986. *The Italian Renaissance: Culture and Society in Italy*. Princeton, N. J.: Princeton University Press.

———. 1987. *The Historical Anthropology of Early Modern Italy*. Cambridge: Cambridge University Press.

Calabrese, Stefano. 1984. *Gli Arabeschi della fiaba: Dal Basile ai romantici*. Pisa: Pacini Editore.

Calmo, Andrea. 1580. *Delle lettere di M. Andrea Calmo*. Books 1–4. Venice: Camillo Pincio. Copy in Beinecke Library, Yale University.

Canepa, Nancy, ed. 1997. *Out of the Woods: The Origins of the Literary Fairy Tale in Italy and France*. Detroit: Wayne State University Press.

———. 1999. *From Court to Forest: Giambattista Basile's* Lo cunto de li cunti *and the Birth of the Literary Fairy Tale*. Detroit: Wayne State University Press.

Castiglione, Baldassar. 1528/1903. *The Book of the Courtier*. Trans. Leonard Eckstein Opdycke. New York: Charles Scribner's Sons.

Chambers, David and Brian Pullan, with Jennifer Fletcher, eds. 1992. *Venice: A Documentary History, 1450–1630*. Oxford: Blackwell.

Chojnacki, Stanley. 1994. "Subaltern Patriarchs: Bachelors in Renaissance Venice." In *Medieval Masculinities: Regarding Men in the Middle Ages*, ed. Clare A. Lees. Minneapolis: University of Minnesota Press. 75–90.

———. 2000. *Women and Men in Renaissance Venice: Twelve Essays on Patrician Society*. Baltimore: Johns Hopkins University Press.

Clausen-Stolzenburg, Maren. 1995. *Märchen und mittelalterliche Literaturtradition*. Heidelberg: C. Winter.

Clements, Robert J. and Joseph Gibaldi. 1977. *Anatomy of the Novella: The European Tale Collection from Boccaccio and Chaucer to Cervantes*. New York: New York University Press.

Coseriu, Annemaria. 1987. "Zensur und Literatur in der italienischen Renaissance des XVI. Jahrhunderts: Baldassar Castigliones *Libro del Cortigiano* als
Paradigma." In *Literatur zwischen immanenter Bedingtheit und äusseren
Zwang: Zwei Studien zum Cinquecento*, ed. Alfred Noyer-Weidner. Roman-
ica Monacensia 26. Tübingen: Gunter Narr.

Cottino-Jones, Margo. 1994. *Il Dir novellando: Modelle e deviazione*. Rome:
Salerno.

———. 2000. "Princesses, Frogs, and the Fantastic." *Italian Quarterly* 37: 173–84.

Davis, James C. 1975. *A Venetian Family and Its Fortune, 1500–1900: The Donà and
the Conservation of Their Wealth*. Philadelphia: American Philosophical
Society.

Davis, Robert C. 1991. *Shipbuilders of the Venetian Arsenal: Workers and Workplace in the Preindustrial City*. Baltimore: Johns Hopkins University Press.

———. 1994. *The War of the Fists: Popular Culture and Public Violence in Late
Renaissance Venice*. New York: Oxford University Press.

De Filippis, Michele. 1947. "Straparola's Riddles." *Italica* 24, 2 (1947): 134–46.

Delille, Gérard. 1996. "Strategie di alleanza e demografia del matrimonio." In
Storia del matrimonio, ed. Michela De Giorgio, Christiane Klapisch-Zuber,
and Marina Beer. Roma-Bari: Laterza. 283–303.

Demnati, Faouzia. 1989. *Le Merveilleux et le réalisme et leurs implications sociales et
culturelles dans les "Piacevoli Notti" de Giovan Francesco Straparola*. Publications de la Faculté des lettres de Manouba, Série Lettres 3; Manouba
(Tunisia): Faculté des Lettres.

Dijstelberge, Paul. 1997. "Introduction to the Catalogue of Works Published
Before 1800." In *Plague and Print in the Netherlands: A Short-Title Catalogue of Publications in the University Library of Amsterdam*, ed. Dijstelberge
and L. Noordegraaf. Rotterdam: Erasmus. 11–17.

Doni, Anton Francesco. 1552. *I Marmi del Doni, academico peregrino: Al Mag^{er} et
Eccellente S. Antonio de Feltro dedicati. Con privilegio*. Venice: Francesco
Marcolini.

———. 1557. *La Libraria del Doni fiorentino*. Venice: Gabriel Giolito de' Ferrari.
Copy in Beinecke Library, Yale University.

———. 1575. *Mondi celesti, terrestri, et infernali, de gli accademici pellegrini*. Venice:
Domenico Farri. Copy in Beinecke Library, Yale University.

Donvito, Vincenza. 1997. "Comin da Trino." In *Dizionario dei tipografi e degli
editori italiani: Il Cinquecento*, ed. Marco Menato, Ennio Sandal, and
Giuseppina Zappella. Milan: Editrice Bibliografica.

Duncan-Jones, Katherine. 2001. *Ungentle Shakespeare: Scenes from His Life*. London: Arden Shakespeare.

Dunlop, John Colin. 1816. *The History of Fiction: Being a Critical Account of the
Most Celebrated Prose Works of Fiction, from the Earliest Greek Romances to the
Novels of the Present Age*. London: Longman, Hurst, Rees, Orme, and Brown.

Dürer, Albrecht. 1913. *Record of Journeys to Venice and the Low Countries*. Ed.
Roger Fry. Boston: Merrymount Press.

*Enzyklopädie des Märchens: Handwörterbuch zur historischen und vergleichenden
Erzählforschung*.1977–. Berlin: Walter de Gruyter.

Escarpit, Denise. 1985. *Histoire d'un conte: Le chat botté en France et en Angleterre*. Paris: Didier Érudition.

Franco, Veronica. 1998. *Poems and Selected Letters*. Ed. Anne Rosalind Jones and Margaret F. Rosenthal. Chicago: University of Chicago Press.

Gilbert, Felix. 1973. "Venice in the Crisis of the League of Cambrai." In *Renaissance Venice*, ed. J. R. Hale. London: Faber and Faber. 274–92.

Giquel, Bernard. 1998. "Les *Contes* de Perrault: Réception critique et histoire littéraire." In *Tricentenaire Charles Perrault: Les grands contes du XVII^c siècle et leur fortune littéraire*, ed. Jean Perrot. Paris: In Press. 111–22.

Gonzenbach, Laura. 1870. *Sicilianische Märchen: Aus dem Volksmund gesammelt*. Leipzig: W. Engelmann.

Grafton, Anthony. 1985. "Renaissance Readers and Ancient Texts: Comments on Some Commentaries." *Renaissance Quarterly* 38, 4: 615–49.

Grendler, Paul E. 1977. *The Roman Inquisition and the Venetian Press, 1540–1605*. Princeton, N.J.: Princeton University Press.

———. 1989. *Schooling in Renaissance Italy: Literacy and Learning, 1300–1600*. Baltimore: Johns Hopkins University Press.

———. 1995. "What Piero Learned in School: Fifteenth-Century Vernacular Education." In *Piero della Francesca and His Legacy*, ed. Marilyn Aronberg Lavin. Hanover, N.H.: University Press of New England.

Griffante, Caterina. 1994. "Esopo tra Medio Evo ed Umanesimo." *Lettere Italiane* 46, 2: 315–40.

Grimm, Jacob and Wilhelm Grimm. 1822, 1856/1980. *Brüder Grimm: Kinder- und Hausmärchen*. Ed. Heinz Rölleke. Stuttgart, Reclam. 3: 285–90.

Gueroult, Guillaume, trans. 1553. *Epitome de la Corographie d'Europe*. Lyons: Balthazar Arnoullet. Copy in Houghton Library, Harvard University.

Guglielminetti, Marziano. 1979. "Dalle 'Novellae' del Morlini alle 'Favole' dello Straparola." In *Medievo e Rinascimento Veneto con altri studi in onore di Lino Lazzarini: Dal Cinquecento al Novecento*. Padua: Editrice Antenore. 69–81.

———. 1984. *La Cornice e il furto: studi sulla novella del '500*. La parola letteraria 7. Bologna: Zanichelli.

Gullino, Giuseppe. 1994. "Quando il mercante costrui la villa: Le proprietò dei Veneziani nella Terraferma." In *Storia di Venezia dalle Origini alla Caduta della Serenissima*, vol. 6, *Dal Rinascimento al Barocco*, ed. Gaetano Cozzi and Paolo Prodi. Rome: Istituto della Enciclopedia Italiana. 875–924.

Hanawalt, Barbara. 1993. *Growing Up in Medieval London: The Experience of Childhood in History*. New York: Oxford University Press.

Hannon, Patricia. 1988. "Feminine Voice and the Motivated Text: Madame d'Aulnoy and the Chevalier de Mailly." *Marvels & Tales* 2, 1 (1988): 13–24.

Historia di Lionbruno. 1476/1976. Toronto: Toronto Public Library.

Hosch, Reinhard. 1986. "Eine unbekannte Quelle und biographische Hintergründe zur Geschichte des schönen Bettlers in Brentanos 'Urchronika'." *Jahrbuch des Freien Deutschen Hochstifts*: 216–33.

Imbriani, Vittorio. 1877. *La novellaja fiorentina: Fiabe e novelline stenografate in Firenze dal dettato popolare*. Livorno: F. Vigo.

Klotz, Volker. 1985. *Das europäische Kunstmärchen*. Stuttgart: Metzler.

Köhler-Zülch, Ines. 1991. "Ostholsteins Erzählerinnen in der Sammlung Wilhelm Wissers: ihre Texte—seine Berichte." *Fabula* 32: 94–118.

Labalme, Patricia H. 1980. "Women's Roles in Early Modern Venice: An Exceptional Case." In *Beyond Their Sex: Learned Women of the European Past*, ed. Labalme. New York: New York University Press. 129–52.

Lane, Frederic Chapin. 1934/1973. *Venetian Ships and Shipbuilders of the Renaissance*. Baltimore: Johns Hopkins University Press.

———. 1965. *Navires et constructeurs à Venise pendant la Renaissance*. Paris: E. Touzot.

Larivaille, Paul. 1973/1979. *Perspectives et limites d'une analyse morphologique du Conte: Pour une révision du schéma de Propp*. Paris: Centre de Recherches de Langue et Littérature Italiennes.

Leclerc, Marie-Dominique. 1993. "Le Sentiment religieux dans l'oeuvre de Pierre de Larivey." *Mémoires de la Société Académique de l'Aube* 117: 23–57.

Logan, Oliver. 1972. *Culture and Society in Venice, 1470–1790: The Renaissance and Its Heritage*. New York: Charles Scribner's Sons.

Lommatzsch, Erhard. 1950–63. *Beiträge zur älteren italienischen Volksdichtung: Untersuchungen und Texte*. 4 vols. Berlin: Akademieverlag.

Lowry, Martin C. 1992. "Magni Nominis Umbra? L'editoria classica da Aldo Manuzio Vecchio ad Aldo Giovane." In *La Stampa in Italia nel Cinquecento*, ed. Marco Santoro. Rome: Bulzoni Editore. 237–53.

Magnanini, Suzanne. 2000. "Between Fact and Fiction: The Representation of Monsters and Monstrous Births in the Fairy Tales of Gianfrancesco Straparola and Giambattista Basile." PhD dissertation, University of Chicago.

Martin, Ruth. 1989. *Witchcraft and the Inquisition in Venice, 1550–1650*. Oxford: Blackwell.

Martone, Valerie and Robert Martone. 1994. *Renaissance Comic Tales of Love, Treachery, and Revenge*. New York: Italica Press.

Mazzacurati, Giancarlo. 1971. *Società e strutture narrative (dal Trecento al Cinquecento)*. Naples: Liguori Editore.

———. 1996. *All'ombra di Dioneo: Tipologie e percorsi della novella da Boccaccio a Bandello*. Florence: La Nuova Italia.

Mazzi, A. 1909. "Un ex libris di G. F.Straparola." *Bolletino della Biblioteca civica di Bergamo* 4: 155–56.

Moro, Giacomo, ed. 1989. *Novo libro di lettere scritte da i più rari auttori e professori della lingua volgare italiana: Ristampa anastatica delle edd. Gherardo, 1544 e 1545*. Istituto di Studi Rinascimentali-Ferrara Libri di Lettere del Cinquecento 4. Ferrara: Arnaldo Forni Editore.

Mortier, Alfred. 1930. *Études italiennes*. Paris: Messein.

Mortimer, Ruth. 1996. "The Author's Image: Italian Sixteenth-Century Printed Portraits." *Harvard Library Bulletin* n.s. 7, 2: 7–87.

Motte, Anne. 1972. "La Thème de la beffa dans les Piacevoli Notti de Giovanfrancesco Straparola." In *Formes et significations de la "Beffa" dans la littérature italienne de la Renaissance*, ed. André Rochon. 2 vols. Centre de Recherche sur la Renaissance Italienne 1, 4. Paris: Université de la Sorbonne Nouvelle. 167–77.

Muir, Edward. 1981. *Civic Ritual in Renaissance Venice*. Princeton, N.J.: Princeton University Press.

Ovid (Publius Ovidius Naso). 1508. *Methamorphoses vulgare hystoriado*. Trans. Giovanni Bonsignore. Venice: Alessandro Bindoni for Luc Antonio Giunto.

Padoan, Giorgio. 1985. "Su un nono 'plagio'plautino-ruzantescoi Lodovico Dolce." In *Culture et société en Italie du Moyen Age à la Renaissance*, ed. André Rochon. Paris: Université dela Sorbonne Nouvelle.

Perocco, Daria, ed. 1985. *Lettere da diversi re e principe e cardinali e altri uomini dotti a mons, Pietro Bembo scritte: Ristampa anastatica dell'ed. Sansovino, 1560*. Istituto di Studi Rinascimentali, Lettere del Cinquecento 1. Ferrara: Arnaldo Forni, 1985.

Perrot, Jean, ed. 1998. *Tricentenaire Charles Perrault: Les grands contes du XVIIe siècle et leur fortune littéraire*, Paris: In Press.

Piejus, Marie-Françoise. 1976. "Le Couple citadin-paysan dans les 'Piacevoli notti' de Straparola." In *Ville et campagne dans la littérature italienne de la Renaissance*, ed. André Rochon. Paris: Université de la Sorbonne.139–77.

Petrini, Mario. 1983. *La Fiaba di magia nella letteratura italiana*. Udine: Del Bianco Editore.

Pirovano, Donato. 2000. "Una storia editoriale cinquecentesca: 'Le piacevoli notti' di Giovan Francesco Straparola." *Giornale storico della letteratura italiana* 177: 540–69.

———. 2001. "Per l'edizione de *Le Piacevoli notti* di Giovan Francesco Straparola." *Filologia e Critica* 26: 60–93.

Pitrè, Giuseppe. 1986. *Giuseppe Pitrè: Märchen aus Sizilien*. Ed. Rudolf Schenda and Doris Senn. Munich: Diederichs.

Pozzi, Victoria Smith. 1981. "Straparola's 'Le piacevoli notti': Narrative technique and Ideology." PhD dissertation, UCLA.

Pullan, Brian. 1971. *Rich and Poor in Renaissance Venice: The Social Institutions of a Catholic State to 1620*. Oxford: Blackwell.

———. 1973. "Occupations and Investment of the Venetian Nobility in the Middle and Late Sixteenth Century." In *Renaissance Venice*, ed. J. R. Hale. London: Faber and Faber. 379–408.

———. 1999. "Town Poor, Country Poor: The Province of Bergamo from the Sixteenth to the Eighteenth Century." In *Medieval and Renaissance Venice*, ed. Ellen E. Kittell and Thomas F. Madden. Urbana: University of Illinois Press. 213–36.

Quondam, Amedeo. 1977. "Mercanzia d'honore, mercanzia d'utile: produzzione libraria e lavoro intelletuale a Venezia nel '500." In *Libri, editori e pubblico nell'Europa moderna: Guida storico-critica*, ed. Armando Petrucci. Rome: Laterza. 51–104.

Rapp, Richard T. 1976. *Industry and Economic Decline in Seventeenth-Century Venice*. Cambridge, Mass.: Harvard University Press.

Richardson, Brian. 1994. *Print Culture in Renaissance Italy: The Editor and the Vernacular Text, 1470–1600*. Cambridge: Cambridge University Press.

———. 1999. *Printing, Writers, and Readers in Renaissance Italy*. Cambridge: Cambridge University Press.

Rizzardi, Simona. 1989. "Le *Piacevoli notti* di Giovan Francesco Straparola e le 'commedie elegiache' latine medievali." In *Moving in Measure: Essays in Honour of Brian Moloney*, ed. Judith Bryce and Doug Thompson. Hull: Hull University Press. 63–77.

Rosenthal, Margaret F. 1992. *The Honest Courtesan: Veronica Franco, Citizen and Writer in Sixteenth-Century Venice*. Chicago: University of Chicago Press.

Rua, Giuseppe. 1890a. "Intorno alle 'Piacevoli Notti' dello Straparola." *Giornale storico della letterature italiana* 15: 111–51.

———. 1890b. "Intorno alle 'Piacevoli Notti' dello Straparola." *Giornale storico della letterature italiana* 16: 218–83.

———. 1898. *Le 'Piacevoli notti' di Messer Gian Francesco Straparola: Ricerche di Giuseppe Rua*. Rome: E. Loescher.

Rubini, Luisa. 1998. *Fiabe e mercanti in Sicilia: La raccolta di Laura Gonzenbach, la comunità di lingua tedesca a Messina nell'Ottocento*. Florence: Leo S. Olschki Editore.

Ruggiero, Guido. 1985. *The Boundaries of Eros: Sex, Crime, and Sexuality in Renaissance Venice*. New York: Oxford University Press.

———. 1993. *Binding Passions: Tales of Magic, Marriage, and Power at the End of the Renaissance*. New York: Oxford University Press.

Salinari, Giambattista. 1955. *Novelle del Cinquecento*. Turin, Unione Typografico-Editrice.

Santagiuliana, Tullio. 1981. *Caravaggio: Profilo storico*. Treviglio: Signorelli.

Scaperotta, Genny. 2000. *Guida alla Chiesa Parrocchiale di Caravaggio*. Caravaggio: Scuola Media "La Sorgente."

Secco D'Aragona, Fermo. 1968. *Storia di Caravaggio e Isola Fulcheria: Narrata dai documenti del suoi signori e condottieri*. Brescia: Appolonia.

Senn, Doris. 1993. "*Le piacevoli Notti* (1550/53) von Giovan Francesco Straparola, ihre italienische Editionen und die spanische Übersetzung *Honesto y agradable Entretenimiento de Damas y Galanes* (1569/81) von Francisco Truchado." *Fabula* 34: 45–65.

Smarr, Janet Levarie, ed. 1983. *Italian Renaissance Tales*. Rochester Mich.: Solaris.

Straparola, Giovanfrancesco (Zoan Francesco). 1508. *Opera nova de Zoan Francesco Straparola da Caravazo, novamente stampata: Sonetti cxv, Strambotti xxxv, Epistole vii, Capitoli xii*. Venice: Georgio de Ruschoni. Copy in British Library, G 10747.

———. 1515. *Opera nova de Zoan Francesco Straparola da Caravazo, novamente stampata: Sonetti cxvii, Strambotti xxxv, Epistole vii, Capitoli xii*. Venice: Alexandro di Bindoni. Copy in Marquand Library, Princeton University.

———. 1550 (1551). Book 1. *Le Piacevoli Notti di M. Giovan Francesco Straparola da Caravaggio. Nelle qvali si contengono le fauole con i loro enimmi da dieci donne, & duo giouani raccontate, cosa diletteuole he piu data in luce*. Con Privilegio. Venice: Appresso Orpheo dalla carta tien per insegna S. Aluise (Comin da Trino di Monferrato). Copies in Houghton Library, Harvard University and Beinecke Library, Yale University.

———. 1551. *Le Piacevoli Notti di M. Giovan Francesco Straparola da Caravaggio. Nelle qvali si contengono le fauole con i loro enimmi da dieci donne, & duo giouani raccontate, cosa diletteuole he piu data in luce.* Book 1. Con Privilegio. Venice: (Comin da Trino di Monferrato) A San Luca al segno del Diamante. Copy in Cotsen Library, Princeton University.

———. 1553. *Le Piacevoli notti di M. Giovanfrancesco Straparola da Caravaggio. Nelle qvali si contengono le fauole con e lor (sic) enigmi (sic) da dieci donne raccontate, cosa diletteuole, ne piu data in luce. Libro secondo. Con Privilegio.* Venice: A San Bartholameo alla libraria della colombina. M.D.LIII. (Comin da Trino). Copy in Beinecke Library, Yale University.

———. 1555. *Le Piacevoli Notti di M. Giovanfrancesco Straparola da Carauaggio. Nelle quali si contengono le fauole con i loro enimmi da dieci donne, & duo giociani raccontate, cosa diletteuole, ne piu data in luce. Libro primo. Con Privilegio.* Venice: Appresso Orfeo dalla Carta tien per insegna S. Aluise. M.D.LV (Comin da Trino). Copy in Beinecke Library, Yale University.

———. 1556. *Le Piacevoli Notti di M. Giovan Francesco Straparola da Caravaggio. Nelle qvali si contengono le fauole con i loro enimmi da dieci donne, & duo giouani raccontate, cosa diletteuole ne piu data in luce.* Venice: Appresso Orfeo della Carta tien per insegna S. Aluise (Comin da Trino). Copy in Nationalbibliothek, Vienna.

———. 1679. *Degli spiriti generosi. Passatempo Toscano, ciò è ingegniosi enimmi di M. Giovan Francesco Straparola da Caravaggio,* ed. Gabriel Sculteti Onghero. Leipzig: Hans Colero. Copy in British Library, 12316.aa.37(3).

———. 1790. *Copia di un caso notabile intervenuto a un gran gentil'uomo genovese: Cose molto utile da intender et di gran piacere.* Venice: n.p. Copy in British Library.

———. 1857. *Les Facétieuses nuits de Straparole traduites par Jean Louveau et Pierre de Larivey.* Ed. Paul Jannet. Paris: P. Jannet, Bibliothèque Elzévirienne.

———. 1898. *The Facetious Nights of Straparola.* Trans. W. G. Waters, illus. Jules Garnier and E. R. Hughes. 4 vols. London: Society of Bibliophiles.

———. 1899. *Le Piacevoli Notti di M. Giovanfrancesco Straparola da Caravaggio.* Ed. and intro. Giuseppe Rua. Bologna: Presso Romagnoli-call'Acqua.

———. 1908. *Le Piacevoli notti di M. Giovanfrancesco Straparola da Caravaggio.* Ed. and intro Giuseppe Rua. Bologna: Presso Romagnoli-call'Acqua.

———. 1943. *Le Piacevoli notti.* Ed. Giovanni Machia. Milan: Bompiani.

———. 1979. *Straparola: Le Piacevoli notti.* Ed. M. Pastore Stocchi. 2 vols. Rome: Laterza.

———. 1999. *Les Nuits facétieuses.* Ed., trans., and afterword Joël Gayraud. Paris: Librairie José Corti.

———. 2000. *Le Piacevoli notti.* Ed. Donato Pirovano. Rome: Salerno Editrice.

Stussi, Alfredo. 1989. "Scelte linguistiche e connotati regionali nella novella italiana." In *La Novella italiana: Atti del convegno di Caprarola 19–24 settembre 1988.* 2 vols. Rome: Salerno Editrice. 191–214.

Todorov, Tzvetan. 1977. *The Poetics of Prose.* Trans. Richard Howard. Ithaca, N.Y.: Cornell University Press.

Trost, Caroline T. 1991. "'Belle-Belle ou le chevalier Fortuné': A Liberated Woman in a Tale by Mme d'Aulnoy." *Marvels & Tales* 5, 1 (1991): 57–67.

Tucci, Ugo. 1973. "The Psychology of the Venetian Merchant in the Sixteenth

Century." In *Renaissance Venice*, ed. J. R. Hale. London: Faber and Faber. 346–78.

Ughetti, Dante. 1981. "Larivey Traduttore delle 'Piacevoli Notti' di Straparola." In *La Nouvelle française à la Renaissance*, ed. Lionello Sozzi and V. L. Saulnier. Geneva: Slatkine. 481–504.

Villani, Gianni. 1982. "Da Morlini a Straparola: Problemi di traduzione e problemi del testo." *Giornale Storico delle Letteratura Italiana* 159, 505: 67–73.

Vriesema, P. C. A. 1986. "The STCN Fingerprint." *Studies in Bibliography* 39: 93–100.

Zipes, Jack. 1997. "Of Cats and Men." In *The Origins of the Literary Fairy Tale in Italy and France*, ed. Nancy L. Canepa. Detroit: Wayne State University Press. 176–93.

OTHER WORKS CONSULTED

Bellavitis, Giorgio and Giandomenico Romanelli. 1985. *Venezia*. Rome: Editori Laterza.

Bragantini, Renzo. 1987. *Il riso sotto il velame. La novella cinquecentesca tra l'avventura e la norma*, Florence: Leo S. Olschki.

Brown, Judith C. and Robert C. Davis, eds. 1998. *Gender and Society in Renaissance Italy*. London: Longman.

Finlay, Robert. 1980. *Politics in Renaissance Venice*. New Brunswick, N.J.: Rutgers University Press.

Gilbert, Felix. 1980. *The Pope, His Banker, and Venice*. Cambridge, Mass.: Harvard University Press.

Hausman, Frank-Rutger. 1992. *Bibliographie der deutschen Übersetzungen aus dem Italienischen von den Anfängen bis 1730*. Tübingen: Max Niemeyer.

Morin, Louis. 1937. *Les Trois Pierre de Larivey: Biographie et bibliographie*. Troyes: Paton.

Pullan, Brian. 1968. *Crisis and Change in the Venetian Economy in the Sixteenth and Seventeenth Centuries*. London: Methuen.

Straparola, Giovanfrancesco. 1560. *Les Facecievses Nuictz dv Seigneur Ian Francois Straparole: aueq les Fables & Enigmes, racontées par deux ieunes getilshommes, & dix Damoiselles. Nouuellement traduittes d'Italien en François, par Ian Louueau. Aveq privilege du Roy*. Lyon: Par Guillaume Rouille. Copy in Nationalbibliothek, Vienna.

——. 1567. *Le Piacevoli notti di M. Giovan Francesco Straparola da Carauaggio. Nelle qvali si contengono le Favole con i loro Enimmi da dieci donne, & duo giovani raccontate. Nuouamente ristampate & con diligenza rauuedute*. Venice: Appresso Iseppo di Mantelli. Copy in Nationalbibliothek, Vienna.

——. 1570. *Le Tredici iacevoli otti del Sig. Gio. Francesco Straparola da Carauaggio*. Venice: Appresso Domenico Farri. Copy in Nationalbibliothek, Vienna.

——. 1573. *Les Facecievses nvictz dv Seigneur Iean Francois Straparole. Auec les Fables & Enigmes, racontées par deux ieunes gentilzhommes, & dix Damoiselles.*

Nouuellement traduictes d'Italien en François par Iean Louueau. Paris: Imprimerie de Mathurin Martin. Copy in Bibliothèque de l'Arsenal, Paris.

———. 1577. *Le Premier livre des facecievses nuicts. du Seigneur Jean François Straparole. Avec les Fables & Enigmes, racontée par deux ieunes gentilz-hommes & dix Damoiselles. Mouuellement traduictes d'Italien en François par Jean Louueau. De nouveau reuouës, corrigées, & augmentées de chansons au commencement de chacune nuict*. Paris: Pour Abel L'Angelier, tenant sa boutique au premier pilier de la grand salle du Pallais. Copy in Nationalbibliothek, Vienna.

———. 1578. *Honesto y agradable entretenemiento de damas y galanes trad. de lengua Toscana en la nuestra vulgar por Francesco Truchado*. Caragoca [Saragossa]: Soler. Copy in Nationalbibliothek, Vienna.

———. 1584. *Les XIII piacevoli notti del S. Gio. Francesco Straparola, da Caravaggio. Divise in dve libri. Novamente ristampate, & con somma diligenza reuiste, & correcte*. Venice: Appresso Domenico Farri. Copy in Bibliothèque Mazarine, Paris.

———. 1586. *Le Tredici piacevoli notte del S. Gio. Francesco Straparola, da Caravaggio. Divise in Dve libri, nouamente ristampate, & con somma diligenza reuiste & correcte*. Venice: Appresso Domenico Caualcalupo. Copies in Nationalbibliothek, Vienna and Beinecke Library, Yale University.

———. 1597. *Le Tredici piacevoli notte del S. Giovan Francesco Straparola, da Caravaggio, divise in Due libri. Nouamente ristampate, & con somma diligenza reviste & espurgate da tutti quelli errori che in esse si contenevano, con licentia de' superiori*. Venice: Presso Daniel Zanetti. Copy in Nationalbibliothek, Vienna.

———. 1601. *Le Tredici piacevolissime notti di M. Gio Francesco Straparola da Carauaggio … di bellissime Figure adornata …* Venice: Daniel Zanetti. Copy in Universitätsbibliothek, Basel.

———. 1609. *Le Tredici piacevolissime notti di M. Gio Francesco Straparola da Carauaggio … di bellissime Figure adornata …* Venice: Zanetto Zanetti. Copy in Universitätsbibliothek, Basel.

———. 1726. *Les Facecieuses nuicts du Seigneur Straparole*. Paris: Guerin. Copy in Bibliothèque Mazarine, Paris.

Trinicato, Egle and Umberto Franzoi. 1971. *Venezia au fil du temps*. Boulogne-Billancourt: Éditions Joel Cuenot.

Veneziani, Paolo. 1990. "La Marca tipografica di Comin da Trino." *Gutenberg Jahrbuch*: 162–73.

Index

Acknowledgments

As a newcomer to Renaissance Italian history and literature, I have needed, and have greatly profited from, generous help freely given by many colleagues. At Stony Brook, Lori Repetti and Andrea Fedi helped with the translation of Straparola's sonnet, "O Caravaggio." Further afield, Paul Grendler kindly read Chapter 3 and, with his enormous and wide-ranging knowledge of Renaissance social history, saved me from more than one misperception. I hope I haven't added any since he read those pages. It gives me pleasure to be able to thank Brian Richardson at the University of Leeds in print. With enormous generosity, he has endeavored to bring me up to date with the relevant bibliography for the world of print in Renaissance Venice. Suzanne Magnanini at the University of Colorado at Boulder and Doris Senn in Zürich each read individual chapters, querying assumptions that needed clarification, as did an old friend, Maria Tatar, at Harvard. All these readings have measurably improved my efforts.

Over the years I often discussed Straparola with the late Rudolf Schenda in conversations that always ended with notes and references. Everyone who benefited from his wide-ranging knowledge of folk narrative in Italy, France, Germany, and England misses him deeply and knows what a great loss his death has been.

In the course of preparing my manuscript it was inevitable that a book I needed to consult yet again lay hundreds or thousands of miles away. My dear friends Mary Sullivan Flannery and Vincent Carey checked words and pages for me at the British Library and at the Folger Library in Washington, D.C., and I thank them from the bottom of my heart.

Stony Brook's Inter-Library Loan staff achieves miracles in minutes, and I want to thank them, and in particular Donna Sammis, for expert help in securing arcane and obscure publications.

I've visited many libraries in the course of my research, and for their support I would like to thank them here: Bibliothèque de l'Arsenal

(Paris); Bibliothèque Mazarine (Paris); British Library; Nationalbibliothek (Vienna), Biblioteca Communale (Caravaggio); Plantin Moretus Library (Antwerp); libraries of Wellesley College and of the universities of Basel, Harvard, Princeton, and Yale.

As for translations from Straparola, I originally intended to use those of W. G. Waters, but after a hundred years their language is antiquated. Though generally reliable, there are some instances in which his translation does not faithfully represent Straparola's language, and that led me to retranslate all passages that appear here.

Finally there are the thanks that cover so many parts of the scholarly process that they are hard to enumerate. Everyone with a patient companion understands them. For having ideas tested on him, for proofreading manuscripts, and for every domestic inconvenience that long and passionate involvement with a scholarly book entails, I thank Karl Bottigheimer.